South Asian Communities
catalysts for educational change

Sofia Chanda-Gool

Trentham Books
Stoke on Trent, UK and Sterling USA

Trentham Books Limited

Westview House	22883 Quicksilver Drive
734 London Road	Sterling
Oakhill	VA 20166-2012
Stoke on Trent	USA
Staffordshire	
England ST4 5NP	

© 2006 Sofia Chanda-Gool

First published 2006

British Library Cataloguing-in-Publication Data
A catalogue record for this book is available from the British Library

ISBN-10: 1-85856-382-8
ISBN-13: 978-1-85856-3382-4

Designed and typeset by Trentham Print Design Ltd, Chester and printed in Great Britain by Cromwell Press Ltd, Trowbridge.

Contents

This book is dedicated to Tess, Theo and Tashi

Acknowledgements

This book represents a collective endeavour, many clever and inspiring people assisted in different ways. In particular Dr Carol Morgan's thoughtfulness and creative suggestions, Dr Rajani Naidoo's analysis and moral support, Professor David Gillborn's and Dr Roger Ballard's initial prompts and Professor Andrew Pollard's encouragement were fundamental.

All my South Asian friends especially Azmeena, Azmina, Zehra and Ikram, Nirmal Bal, Uma, Nusrat, Amina, Farhana, Balginder and Lisa as well as all the invaluable participants in this study provided the warmth, companionship and liveliness to focus my mind and wake me up to their exciting and moving experiences. T12, especially Dot, Alison, Jan, Lynn, Carol and Liz and all those in the Education Action Zone; Lindsey and Jayne including several schools offered me the opportunity to explore possibilities in the classroom: the children were engaging and delightful to work with. Nancy, Sean, Reni, Judy, Maggie, Mary, Denise, Rachael, Jux, Catty, Pat, Ken, Keith, Suad Yusaf and Aflah members kept me company and shared thoughts; also Emma Agusita's videoing of KARE provides a wonderful record of our work and Klaus Kalde's skill and acuteness brought the cover into being. My extended family including Catherine, Aisha and Nick kept the homes fires burning. Also vital connections in Bangladesh, India and Australia such as Abhik and Indrani Chanda, Lisa's family, Chris Sarra, Uncle Albert Holt, Robert Bush, Deborah Mosely, Robin Khan and Shamsul Haque: all people who provided some initial thoughts and helped me begin to understand other ways of seeing and believing.

I am indebted to Dr Gillian Klein: her perspicacity, attention to detail and enthusiasm lifted my spirits and made this final draft a reality.

1

Introduction

The inner cities of the UK house a vibrant and complex range of South Asian* communities. This book is about several such communities in one city area. They represent a kaleidoscope of values, beliefs and experiences. Often perceived as just 'different' – as Asian, South Asian or Muslim – their distinctiveness can be lost. Instead they have imposed on them a stereotypical identity, which stultifies possibilities of interaction and exchange. But still they resist, adapt, transform and interact with the wider society. They are catalysts for change, moving between continents, absorbing different beliefs and practices as they cross from one culture to another. They influence the wider society and they are influenced by it. As agents of change, they present the UK with other perspectives and expectations of life; their presence challenges the notion of what is 'British'.

The South Asian families in this study prefix any allusion to being British with their home of origin or religious identity: South Asian, Punjabi, Sikh, Bangladeshi, Pakistani, Muslim or Asian. This suggests that a non-UK home of origin may be more affirming; that belonging to somewhere on the other side of the globe may somehow feel more like 'home'. Why this is so and what it may mean is a central focus of this book.

The book distils what these different experiences and beliefs can offer the UK and particularly the educational system. Not in terms of the superficial glamour of popular Bollywood but in terms of existence itself. It explores what sustains meaning for us even when we are surrounded with incompatibilities between where we were and where we are now. However much the West has sought to persuade

1

us that it encapsulates all we desire, the search for a shared humanity and sense of belonging can still elude us. Words such as 'home', 'place' and 'family' can appear clinical rather than comforting. Home does not necessarily convey a sense of hearth or heartland; the concept of place is somewhat transient or abstract and the concept of family is fraught with ambiguity.

This book is about the educational potential in cross-cultural situations. It identifies a clear developmental process for enhancing learning in schools through collaboration between communities and schools to develop children's socio-cognitive/bicultural skills and understanding. The Race Relations (Amendment) Act 2000 has placed a statutory duty on educational institutions to support changes to promote race equality. And the Commission for Race Equality (CRE) *Learning for All* asks whose voice predominates in schools and which voices have still to be heard and integrated into the learning process. This is the time to listen to the communities so we can understand how to engage with transience, change and paradoxical experiences.

When immigrants arrive in a country they bring a value that transcends a tidy set of beliefs and practices. South Asians immigrating to the West bring the experience of difference, disjuncture and a profound sense of attachment to another existence. If this were not so they would not devote almost half their salaries and wealth to returning regularly to the East. They would all be wandering around in the latest fashions and booking package holidays to Majorca. But they are not – their holidays are invariably in South Asia. Mosques and Gurdwaras proliferate and bangra nights are more popular than Christmas or Madonna. South Asian young people want to be South Asian as well as British.

Basit (1997) quotes a young person as saying; 'I want more freedom but not too much'. What does she mean? In the West we aspire to the infinite when it comes to freedom: freedom is our utopia. So for what perverse reason should a young person want 'not too much'? It is this sense of something worth retaining that has the potential to open doors to other aspects of our lives we may too readily dismiss. When a South Asian woman is asked what her religion means to her and she replies 'what's within', how do we understand it?

The book focuses upon the perceptual and emotional issues voiced by South Asian pupils, parents and community representatives and presents the views of two South Asian teachers. Whatever their responses, all the participants except one of the teachers identified themselves as South Asian first and foremost. Three types of response were identified: the reaffirming, the contradictory and compromised, and the dynamic. Parents' and community representatives' responses inevitably affect their children or pupils, the exchange is crucial to how pupils relate to schools.

The home-school context

A child's experience of the transition between home and school can engender an understanding of 'others' and a sense of identification with society's values and beliefs, or alternatively it can challenge the sense of security and meaning that life at home provides. The home/school dynamic will also affect the ease with which children learn at school. This is true for all children but is accentuated for those who come from cultural backgrounds that contrast with the ones that are valued within school.

Although parental engagement is largely acknowledged by the educational system to lie at the heart of educational success, the differences between children's backgrounds and parental resources is not identified (Luthra, 1997; Alldred, David and Edwards, 2001). Parents can be thought of as a homogenous group (Vincent, 2001) who do not represent any particular values, dispositions, or skills. Such parents are not seen to belong to communities nor are their communities clearly related to the educational curriculum or value system. Lack of communication and exchange between schools and South Asian communities has been widely identified (Bhatti, 1999; Sushma Rani Puri, 1997). Parker-Jenkins (1995) reveals the incompatibility between values taught in home and school and Karran (1997) registers the sense of isolation experienced by some communities. The problems persist.

South Asian children's identities are at the centre of cross-cultural tensions, yet the educational system ducks the opportunities to engage with this complex and challenging issue. The repercussions are serious. Higher rates of exclusions for ethnic minority pupils, limited understanding of how different cultural groups experience school, teachers' negative expectations of black pupils (Ghouri, 1998), and a general prejudice towards ethnic minority families and communities within the wider society demand solutions. Institutional racism within the educational system still prevails (Gillborn and Youdell, 2000). Ofsted has responded to this concern and now has to examine whether schools address racism and bullying, including religious harassment experienced by ethnic minority groups and to actively promote appreciation of all pupils' cultures and those of others (Coles, 2003).

Schools are not islands; social contexts merge economic and cultural divisions between school and communities. Pakistani and Bangladeshi families are over represented in the lowest economic band and these social conditions have psychological repercussions. Children who are born into such communities have to cross an invisible chasm when they enter school. School has the potential to broaden horizons or to inhibit progress.

Lack of insight into pupils' homes and their potential contribution to children's educational success can cause pupils to experience a psychic disequilibrium, as if looking into a mirror and seeing nothing there. It is as if the communities and homes do not exist or are of no account. At worst, they are perceived as detrimental to the educational welfare of the child, much as the Australian educational system has devastated Indigenous people's culture and abilities, making some withdraw their children from the system (Gool, 1998). The feelings of alienation and exclusion raised by the parents in the Australian study have some parallels here. Harber (2004) questions whether democracy and children's rights exist in UK schools.

Despite the considerable resources within South Asian communities, their relationship with UK society and the local schools is problematic. Education Action Zones and Excellence in Cities failed to address the education system's lack of knowledge and awareness of communities. Government inclusion policies do not register the degree of separation that still exists between the communities and schools. In general, research tends to reinforce a school-based approach and focus upon school agendas and priorities, regarding the communities as an undifferentiated mass. Studies which look at ethnic minority problems of attainment from this perspective exclude the wider contexts the communities engage in.

For all members of the South Asian communities featured in this book, there exists a feeling of being excluded and a sense of 'belonging' elsewhere. This sense of belonging can transcend the buffeting and cross-cultural tensions created by being South Asian and living in the UK. Beliefs, values, experiences, uncertainties and challenges are embedded within this heartland. The sense of belonging is not just a refuge; it is a belief and a way of being – a space that exists within the communities.

Central to understanding South Asian communities is the recognition of distinctive identities. Identity can be imposed by external influences – how the wider society conceives of a person's identity – or as including the personal source of identity: the assertive, reactive and creative ways in which human beings respond to the outside world. It is this response which is the basis of my research.

Construing identity

Self-identities are comprised of numerous facets, for instance gender, religion, ethnicity and ideology. One Black woman notes that Black women's experience would include a sense of the collective as well as the individual in understanding their identity and she notes the inescapability of ethnic identity. 'For us, there is nothing optional about 'black experience' and/or black studies: we must know ourselves' (Jordan, 1997:560). Recognising a plurality of identities at an intrapersonal level may not, however, take account of the tensions and discontinuities experienced around these competing identities. Billig (1987) notes how people assert their identities in response to particular contexts. He identifies how some people choose to be 'different' as part of their identity within a certain context. For instance, some people act 'ethnically' by identifying with each other and showing the appropriate aspects of themselves such as gestures and opinions. This, asserts Billig, in turn enforces ethnic identity.

Imposed identities

Identity also develops from social interaction, as imposed by others. The social and the intra-personal identity interact, and tensions arise when a person struggles to find compatibility with social context and to develop their identity independently of an imposed identity. Contexts may challenge and undermine or affirm and help to assert one's core identity. This in turn may lead to conflict between the personal and social, so affecting self-esteem and even resulting in cultural or self-rejection (Phinney, 1989). In her study of Bengalis and refugees living in the UK, Patel (1997) analyses the relationship between the social outer identity and the personal inner identity and relates this to the development of self-esteem. Dickinson (1997) notes that both multicultural and antiracist models of society have failed to respond to the needs of young Asian women and that there is a need to acknowledge the female perspective within the specific context experienced by Asian women.

Rampton (1995) registers the issue of social legitimacy that has to be negotiated. 'Interaction needs to be situated in the larger structures that both constrain and are reproduced through specific activities, values, norms, roles, purposes and systems of stratification ... no domain can be studied in isolation: daily life moves across a number, transporting expectations and practices rooted in one domain across to another...' (p348). Cultural identities are dynamic and diverse, situated in and interacting with a variety of contexts and circumstance. Circumstances are also construed by the media and may become constraints.

Stereotyping

Stereotyping is a particular way of imposing an identity. Ethnic minorities lack institutional credibility as they often face pathological views of their community's identity, ie they are seen as deficient groups (see Vincent, 1992; Modood, 1997; Gillborn and Gipps, 1996). This stereotypical view is reinforced by a perceived difference that threatens 'what is normal'. As Stanfield (1994:182) observes: 'no matter how people of color define themselves, there are still the more powerful stereotypes embedded in public culture that define their status and identities within the cosmos of the dominant'. In her novel, *White Teeth*, Smith (2000) describes what it is like to be a 'Paki':

> He, Millet, was a Paki no matter where he came from ... he smelt of curry; had no sexual identity; took other people's jobs; or had no job and bummed off the state; or gave jobs to his relatives...[and] he should go back to his own country ... In short he had no face in this country; no voice in the country. (p234)

Stereotyping severely undermines the complexity and diversity of different cultures and identities. Simplifying potential differences can be a way of marginalising certain groups rather than acknowledging their validity, diversity and ability to change. In his analysis of categories, Lakoff (1987) illustrates how the prototype in a category may fail to represent the range within it. The western world and globalisation can be seen as attempting to simplify and homogenise identities. This denies the fact that groups themselves are diverse.

In the context of South Asian communities there is a complex range of possible responses emanating from identities relating to diverse geographies, histories, cultures, personal experiences and socio-political influences. The responses identified in this book have been narrowed down to three fundamental types, but all are recognised as relating to context. The reaffirming response reflects the sense of belonging to being South Asian in an affirming way. But contexts may also influence people to respond in a contradictory and compromised manner. These responses express a sense of alienation, pain and confusion. Such responses can be located within educational and social contexts that constrain. The dynamic response reflects the sense of belonging coupled with being bicultural and dynamic about the cross-cultural situation experienced.

It is vital to understand the communities from *their* position and learn from their insights, rather than fit a top-down, quantitative analysis of the situation into the general educational concerns policy-makers focus upon. A more general quantitative evaluation prioritises other issues as having overall urgency, for instance the general academic under-attainment across cultural and social divides within the UK. The communities themselves are implicitly involved in any possible progress. They interpret the meaning of education for their children; their responses are crucial to addressing any inadequacies in educational achievement. But understanding is closely related to how we access knowledge and information. What this book reveals is the outcome of a particular approach and process of data collection that placed the participants centre stage. My ethnographic approach was crucial to gathering the rich and complex material. At a fundamental level the participants also influenced the conceptual framework for this study. For example, I noted the diagram in which a South Asian social worker interviewed in the early stages of the fieldwork showed where school was placed among the priorities of South Asian parents. His diagram also indicates that South Asian identities embed religious and cultural dimensions within a communal, collectivist paradigm.

Figure 1.1: The South Asian social worker's diagram

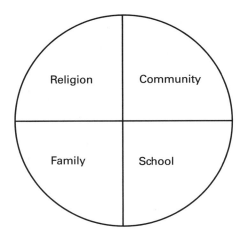

The qualitative approach

The book is based upon a qualitative study of a range of South Asian communities in an inner city area of the UK. The study used a participant centred analysis, or grounded approach, which allows the categories of response to emanate from what the participants said rather than being imposed. It concentrates upon an insider's perspective to learn more about the specific ways in which South Asian identities may be developing. In *To Kill a Mocking Bird*, Lee remarks: 'You never really understand a person until you consider things from his point of view ... until you climb into his skin and walk around a bit ' (1963: 35). An ethnographic approach strives for this, paying particular attention to the influence of the researcher or outsider and to the participants' position and perspectives.

The research experience was enriched by negotiation and involvement with schools and communities through race equality work. Drawing upon the communal strength that characterises these communities, and the learning potential in schools, it was possible to establish a more structured relationship. The inspiration derived from working with the South Asian communities set the precedent for creating links with other communities and developing community based educational initiatives. The underlying aims were to enhance children's achievements, engagement and motivation to learn. The development of BME (Black and Minority Ethnic) discussion groups in schools, educational advisory 'KARE' groups led by the communities; *Kaamyaabi* (led by the South Asian communities) and *Aflah* (led by Black African communities) and the Roots to Empowerment and Achievement Programme (for dual heritage pupils) have all presented opportunities for the communities to act as catalysts for educational change.

The next chapter briefly introduces the research – the approach and the participants. The following four use the three core responses to explore what was discovered in the communities. The reaffirming response is considered in chapter three and the contradictory and compromised response in chapter four. As this second response relates to the home-school situation, the fifth chapter explores this situation through the eyes of the teachers, as contrasted with the communities' responses. The dynamic response is discussed in chapter six. All these responses relate to the potential for exchange and communication. Chapters three, four and six include suggestions for application in the classroom: lesson plans, activities and materials for teachers to augment a shared developmental process. The suggestions have a theoretical premise drawn from the three key responses identified in the research. The concluding chapter summarises the earlier chapters but it also registers that the wider society and social structures, including those in the school, can inhibit development and it offers some examples of practice to overcome this. The afterword reflects upon the ethnographic method and considers how it can be applied as a guide for teachers approaching and liaising with the communities.

It is important to understand what is going on in the communities so we can begin to comprehend the issues that arise for South Asian pupils and parents in the UK. This book explores the experiences and perceptions expressed by the communities. It identifies possible ways in which the communities' contributions can be actively embedded in school education to enhance understanding, meaningfulness, socio-cognitive, bicultural skills and knowledge for the whole school community.

Note

* The term 'South Asian' rather than Asian is clarified by Mirza, 1998: 'Those who define their heritage and/or ethnic origins as from the South Asian subcontinent, which incorporates Bangladesh, India and Pakistan, and includes East African Asians. This does not mean that the differences between and within each group based on, for instance, class, caste and religion, are not recognised. The term is merely used for convenience (p.93).' In this study the participants come from the latter three areas, the Indians/Sikhs coming from the Punjab.

2

South Asian participants and the educational model

> The ethnographer['s] secondary, mediated knowledge may be useful, public, accessible and interesting but it is necessarily dependent and derivative ... What ethnography can contribute is a discipline unravelling the breadth and complexity of relations ... (Rock, 2001: 31)

> It is the mark of a civilised society to aim at eliminating such inequalities as have their source not in individual differences, but in its own organisation; and that individual energies, which are the source of social energy, are more likely to ripen and find expression if social inequalities are, as far as practical diminished. (Tawney, 1964: 57)

I set out to discover how South Asian parents, pupils and families experienced the educational system. I wanted to know what their constructs of success were and how these compared to the local schools' constructs. This ambition may sound interesting in theory: in practice it was like trying to fit an ocean into a fridge. The parts were incompatible. The diversity and contrasts within the communities had to be comprehended before I could see potential connections with schools. I started inductively, bottom-up, changed direction several times, surfaced and, inspired by members of the communities, I found fascinating links that could be framed within school curriculum opportunities.

Key protagonists

I chose participants who felt a strong affiliation to being South Asian, were adept at analysing their values and beliefs and yet able to articulate the cross-cultural tensions they encountered. I coded them according to the responses they offered about the predictable themes of religion, family, culture, education and community that were their priorities. It became apparent that identity was a powerful current running throughout the various themes, affecting their meaning. People owned their interpretation of these themes and were eager to discriminate between the various communities that existed: what existed outside the school was not a single community. Words like *we* rather than *I* predominated, emphasing the shared ownership of identity and culture. It contrasted with the individualism underlying western interpretations of family relations and religious choice.

Approach

My approach was crucial to eliciting the quality of the responses people offered; it was as important as the findings I have recorded. South Asian communities are constantly challenged by the prejudice in the wider society. Negative stereotyping and ignorance of cultural diversity mean their contributions to UK society are denied. There appeared to be a protective shield around their lives and engagements that might help sustain their values and beliefs but which made contact from an outsider tenuous. It took time, determination and expressing great respect for their perspectives and experiences to develop a connection and to be trusted in their world. I embarked on a large learning curve and am indebted to the communities' time, trust, generosity and hospitality. Despite the challenges it was all worth it. Through my engagement and dialogue with the communities, I discovered more about myself and western society than I could have anticipated. Through this experience I learned about the contrast, creativity, anguish, isolation and the pride and joy people experienced. I also gained powerful insight into the diverse knowledge and understanding people had developed. As Gillborn argues (1998), participants who belong to disadvantaged groups are often far more knowledgeable and insightful about their lives than researchers recognise.

To acknowledge and value the wisdom and insight participants contribute, this study has integrated their perspectives and vision into the conceptual framework and the methods as outlined in chapter seven. Their perspectives, commitment to change and collaboration have driven new developments with schools as indicated throughout the book. My approach combined participatory involvement with the communities and a participant led approach as detailed in chapter eight. This aimed to address the imbalance of power, which generally rests with the researcher. I designed my research to incorporate the range of perspectives I discovered, which meant I had to think carefully who I chose to work with. The focus moved from parents to community representatives. These changes are discussed in detail in chapter eight.

A sample of parents had been taken to represent the three South Asian groups identified by the groups themselves: as Bangladeshi, Pakistani and Sikh. But it soon became clear that some of the participants I initially chose were not always representative. To gain a more representative insight into the communities I had to incorporate their cultural and religious diversity. In Stanfield's words, there is a 'need to confess human biases up front and a need to create paradigms grounded in experiences of people of color' (1994: 185).

Coding the participants

The participants are coded first to convey the sense of difference in how each of them chose to prioritise their cultural and religious identity – first as Pakistani or Sikh. Second, they are coded to register the position they took in relation to their own communities. Third, they are analysed in relation to their particular expression of feelings and responses to being South Asian and living within the cross-cultural context of the UK.

I gave the participants letters and numbers rather than names. This was as much for ensuring representation as to ensure anonymity. The coding was specifically designed to register the variation of perspectives in each community rather than indiscriminate community membership.

The nine key representatives

The final nine interviewees do more than represent their own views and knowledge. They have been carefully selected to represent different elements in their communities: the spokesperson, the member and the radical. The Bangladeshi participants have the letter 'B' as part of their identity, the Pakistani participants the letter 'P' and the Sikh participants the letter 'S' plus the numbers 1 for spokesperson, 2 for member, and 3 for radical.

The three representatives chosen for each of the ethnic groups as follows:

Spokesperson: known worker in a community base – identifiable as such

Member: not in the position of spokesperson but nonetheless articulate

Radical: someone who is prepared to speak independently of his or her community

The spokespersons were the officially nominated representatives of a community by common consent of those spoken to in the local area who registered the positive and negative aspects of life in the communities. They also took responsibility for dealing with issues and difficulties as they arose and showed pragmatism and determination to find solutions and to articulate on behalf of the community they represented. By contrast, the members expressed loyalty and affiliation with the community they belonged to but were inclined to be more passive about problematic issues. The radicals, like the members, voiced the concerns and limitations of their communities but could also assert their own way of tackling problems independently of their community, invariably relying upon other resources, sometimes drawn from outside the community, sometimes from their own family and, most conspicuously, themselves.

To add colour and background to these letters and numbers each of the representatives is described below. They are presented in the order in which they occur in the next chapter, although the last (S3) only appears in the third, dynamic response, in chapter six.

B1

This *spokesperson* came to live in the UK when she was four years old. She had an arranged marriage but asserted her rights about exactly who she was prepared to marry. She has a high regard for her parents and meets them daily. Now married and with one child, she has adopted the traditional shalwar kameez. She believes in her Bangladeshi culture and religion and is a confident clear-headed woman who enjoys the responsibility of running a centre.

B2

This *member* was born in the UK and had a fairly disrupted childhood attending several different schools. At fifteen her father insisted that she learn Arabic and Bengali. She had an arranged marriage and has three children. She is very aware of the tensions that exist across cultures and deeply loyal to her community and Bangladeshi identity. She is very reflective and independently minded, although she defers to both her husband's and her father's judgements.

B3

This *radical* lived in Bangladesh until the age of ten and her English is stilted. She has two children and is divorced from her violent husband. Her experience of being a divorcee made her separate from the Bangladeshi community in the area. She expresses an ambivalent attitude towards Bangladeshi culture and states that she is 'Asian'. At times she avoids committing herself to her Bangladeshi origins but emphasises instead the importance of Islam and also education. She is adventurous and independent minded.

S1

This *spokesperson* was born in the UK but her family are close to their extended family in the Punjab and she usually visits them every year with her parents, her husband and her two children. She is deeply religious, yet her vocation as a nurse has made her realise connections with other Asians and non-religious English families. She feels passionately about education and guidance for the younger generation so that they do not lose their connection with Sikhism and yet learn to use the opportunities available to them in the UK. She is assertive, outspoken and thoughtful.

P3

This *radical* was born in the UK. She is the eldest daughter of a family of four and lives with her parents, for whom she has high respect. She has opted to translate the conventions of Islam and Pakistani culture in her own terms and is critical of some of the smallmindedness she sees in her community. She has a degree and understands that her education has helped her to become increasingly independent but she remains very loyal to her Pakistani identity. Although she does sometimes dress in European clothes for work and college, she is clear about her different values and beliefs. Since this study ended she has had a happy arranged marriage. She is quiet, imaginative and can be forceful.

S2

This *member* was born in the UK. She is a devout Sikh, with two children and good relations with her in-laws, whom she hopes will be able to pass on Sikh values and beliefs to her children. She prefers to live in this area than where she lived before because it has a Sikh community. But she is unhappy about the low socio-economic conditions in the locality and finds elements of the community limited and constraining. She prefers to think and act independently of the community centres. She believes that education is vital for her children and supports the local school but she is concerned about its lack of knowledge of Sikhism. She is reflective and dignified.

P1

This *spokesperson* came to England from Pakistan at the age of five and is close to her extended family in Pakistan. She holds her parents in high regard and they were flexible about some of the more stringent aspects of Pakistani culture: she feels she was given a certain amount of freedom. She has three children and is happily married through an arranged marriage. She is deeply committed to working for the Pakistani communities in the area, has acquired a degree as a mature student and is a reflective person with excellent social skills. She is concerned with maintaining Pakistani cultures and Islam but also adapting to the UK context.

P2

This Pakistani *member* is the only male interviewee among the nine. Born in the UK, he lives with his wife who lived in Pakistan until she had an arranged marriage with him and also his mother and his three children. As a child he had more freedom than his sisters and feels that Pakistani women need to be more emancipated. He expressed a complex range of feelings towards some members of his community, its cultural values and the wider UK culture, since he has experienced racism. He feels strongly about the importance of education and the limitations of the local Muslims yet is a dedicated member of his Pakistani community. He is a thoughtful, independent minded and amicable man.

S3

The *radical* Sikh who demonstrated only one type of response provides an example of independence and South Asian identity combined. In many ways S3 is not representative of the perspectives of the Sikh community in this urban area. She is a professional and has lived in various English cities before settling in this locality. Born in the UK, she lived in a similar Sikh community to the one in which this fieldwork was carried out but she broke away from her family, has travelled and lived in India and found her own husband, a Hindu. She is critical of the limitations of school and what she sees as the small-mindedness of the communities. Despite her criticisms of both she made a conscious decision to live in this area. She is a creative person, writing and painting in her spare time. She holds strong views and acts independently of the communities.

Interviewing the pupils

All the pupils were interviewed in groups for two reasons: first, to ensure they felt confident by being in the majority and secondly, so they could encourage each other to share and develop ideas together.

In a year six class of twenty-seven pupils there were fourteen South Asian pupils. The others were Somali, African Caribbean or White. Ten of the fourteen South Asian pupils interviewed were chosen after discussion with the teacher and my observation. Five were Bangladeshi, four Pakistani and one Sikh. The pupils are identified by the letter C and given numbers: 1-5 (B) for the Bangladeshi participants, 6-9 for the Pakistani pupils followed by (P) 10-12 and (S) for the Sikh pupils. Two of the Sikh children were taken from other classes in years five and four because there were so few Sikh children in the school. The use of letters in brackets to denote their cultural group has been made to clarify the fact that the pupils have no relationship to the adult interviewees already described. In the quoted sections of the transcribed interviews the researcher is referred to as SCG.

The families

Once I had discovered who was respected, I interviewed the families on their religious and cultural knowledge as well as their experiences of living in the UK. This was not only useful for getting to know them but also helped build rapport with the communities' members. When they realised that I was the novice and they the experts they became eager to teach me about their cultural and religious beliefs, to address the failings of my parents, who had, they thought, failed in their responsibility to disseminate this knowledge.

Four Bangladeshi, three Pakistani and four Sikh families were interviewed, eleven in all. The Pakistani and Bangladeshi families were eventually accessed through the communities but none were accessed through the school. The need to find links outside the school gave further indication of the community/school *impasse*. All the Sikh families, however, were accessed through the school.

All the families interviewed had children at the school. Not all of them were in year six, nor were all the pupils part of the interview groups. Only four children in the final interview groups were related to the families I interviewed: three Bangladeshi pupils and one Pakistani. The families and pupils were not treated as nuclear units, but representative views were taken from individuals in each of the three communities. What I wanted was a range of representative perspectives rather than family ties.

The teachers

The two teachers in this study were chosen because they are both of South Asian origin: Teacher X taught at the pilot school and Teacher M at the main school I studied. The schools' headteachers suggested that I approach these teachers because of their common identity with the South Asian pupils. As I was initially particularly interested in studying year six I was very fortunate to have access to teachers of South Asian origin teaching in this year, especially as they were the only South Asian teachers at the schools. Although both, like their colleagues, do not live in the locality, they are both mothers and therefore likely to share concerns about equal opportunity with other ethnic minority parents.

A further layer of analysis

Not only was it useful to select key voices in the three ethnic communities, it also became clear that another way of registering the breadth and mobile nature of responses needed to be identified. The three differing perspectives within each community did not convey the ways in which participants were addressing the problems and difficulties they experienced in relation to wider UK society, and therefore also to the school as a British institution. Participants voiced attachment to their countries of origin as explored in the reaffirming response; anxiety and concerns about their experience in the UK as represented in the contradictory and compromised response and bicultural abilities as revealed in the dynamic responses. Sometimes people's individual views comprised a range of attitudes which belong to more than one of the three responses presented in the following chapters. So these are not case studies but investigations of viewpoints. This final level of analysis created the foundations of a socio-cognitive/cultural developmental process as outlined below. Sections 1, 2, and 3 below provide the conceptual framework for a developmental process set out at the end of chapters three, four and six.

Framework for a developmental process and educational model

1) Foundations of knowledge

Our foundations of knowledge are essential to help structure and make sense of influences that surround us when we are born. We develop categories and priorities. For instance, we discriminate between sounds in the first months of life. An infant can learn any number of languages but after a while the sounds that are used and meaningful become the most audible. This is also true of the interaction between the infant and the social world, which contain history and beliefs introduced by carers. These interpretations become the foundations of our world: what is meaningful for us.

Social discourse between an infant and a carer is potentially creative and dynamic. It demands flexibility and sharing meanings, even if the expectations of sharing and of developing a sense of autonomy may differ across cultures. Tedlock and Mannheim (1995) argue that there is no such thing as a monologue but that all our thoughts belong in a social and therefore *dialogic* world that is never static. Vygotsky (1978) also argued that the social dimension to cognitive development is implicit.

The dialogic world is also variable. Shared understanding is not necessarily developed and creatively exercised. Culture plays a powerful role in defining limits and possibilities in subtle as well as obvious ways. Cultures can inhibit exchanges as well as promote them; they can create barriers to exchange. As social beings, our confidence to explore and question others and ourselves requires interaction between emotional or affective and cognitive skills. Feeling threatened or unheard is hardly likely to make us open to exploration and exchanges. Instead it may cause us to build fortresses of knowledge and belief with which to defend what we fear might be challenged and dismantled. Being able to develop an understanding of others who have different perspectives and practices requires a synthesis of our affective, social and cognitive abilities, and a context that promotes exchange.

As beliefs and meanings are often absorbed and not necessarily critiqued they can go unquestioned and be taken literally as 'fact', even if their implications are ambiguous or opaque. It requires confidence, skill and often guidance to unpack meanings and explore the implications of things we take for granted. We need opportunities to contrast and evaluate what we take for granted. In Piaget's (1973) terms, we require an ability to resolve the challenges new knowledge presents through the process of equilibration. Our inherent plasticity (Piaget, 1980) affords us the innate ability to adapt, create and transform our experiences, so as to understand the ideas of others and reinterpret our worlds. This socio-cognitive ability is often underestimated. For purposes of analysis it is separated into cognitive, social and affective abilities but it is unhelpful to focus only on the cognitive at school, relegating the affective to home life.

Driven by league tables that focus on the attainment of particular cognitive skills, schools may find it difficult to integrate affective dimensions into the learning process. For instance, understanding can be inaccurately isolated as a cognitive ability and empathy as an emotional tool. Yet whether we are reading a text, listening, observing or engaging with others, we are drawing upon both the cognitive and affective in the social. It is the combination of these that allows children to develop their knowledge, to challenge or enhance their initial beliefs and perceptions.

2) Addressing cross-cultural challenges

The diverse social world of school presents an ideal opportunity for the exchange of knowledge, understanding of differences and celebration of diversity. However various factors, such as social and political inequality and the negative stereotyping of ethnic minority people militate against this potential. The Commission for Racial Equality (CRE) *Learning for All* identifies the fundamental need for schools to engage more closely with communities and *reach out*: to seek the communities' opinions and identify members to act as role models in school. It also emphasises the need to make the curriculum more culturally relevant and accessible to the children. But engaging with cross-cultural situations and reappraising initial prejudices requires the ability to disembed (Donaldson, 1978), empathise and draw upon the process of equilibration (Piaget, 1973). This process involves complex cognitive skills that include perceptual flexibility, the ability to discriminate and to evaluate. These skills pertinent in academic subjects such as English and science are also exercised in cross-cultural situations. Knowledge of other cultures activates cognition.

Embedding children's values and meanings within the school curriculum can also excite what Vygotsky (1978) identifies as high level thinking. This process complements bicultural development as set out below. Biculturalism includes an ability to ameliorate cultural differences and address some of the conceptual limitations registered above. By developing bicultural skills knowledge can be transformed from the personal and historical foundations developed when we were young children. Learning about different knowledge offers us a reflexive tool by which to evaluate our own knowledge, and an opportunity to synthesise different beliefs and knowledge and develop new meanings.

An adaptation from Byram's (1998) matrix offers us a structure for this developmental process. It incorporates: understanding, empathising and comparing and contrasting different beliefs and practices as set out in four intercultural competences:

1. Openness: recognising the potential in learning about new/different approaches/beliefs and thereby becoming open towards another culture. Seeing one's own cultural as relative rather than finite in terms of values and beliefs.

2. Decentring and seeking knowledge: seeking out information about another culture and hearing the views from insiders of another culture.

3. Recognising and appreciating the challenges and tensions that exist in cross-cultural situations, for example for someone arriving in the UK with a different culture; and, crucially, the need to empathise.

4. Bringing different meanings together, applying the new knowledge by sharing knowledge; engaging with people from another culture; awareness of what has been learned and integrating this knowledge creatively.

3) Creative transformation of knowledge

Transformation of knowledge compliments the socio-cognitive ability to compare, contrast and systematically evaluate different information and experiences: ultimately to create new knowledge. This process involves the ability to develop abstract reasoning (Piaget, 1973). Teachers can help to *scaffold* (Wood *et al*, 1976) this developmental process. Developing bicultural competence has the potential to increase flexible thinking and creativity.

Application to classroom sessions

These sessions draw upon a developmental process, starting with a focus on the foundations of knowledge and moving on to develop an ability to transform knowledge. Empathy with other's perspectives and experiences and tackling the tensions that arise from differences are part of this process. This awareness and insight can then be enhanced so that pupils learn to synthesis differences, share knowledge and work creatively together to problem solve. Chapters three, four and six each end with two consecutive sessions and activities that match the developmental process.

These sessions need to be interactive and flexible to encourage children to develop their understanding from their own knowledge base. Although suggestions are made, it is vital that teachers feel they can adapt and improvise in relation to the constitution of their particular classes. My own practice has been to use videos and DVDs in each session. We created our own DVDs with archive clips of people like Martin Luther King, Bernie Grant, Nelson Mandela, Malcolm X and Maya Angelou. I have also used the Origins video (see below).

Chapter three draws on the communities' knowledge, personal identity and belonging with others. The two sessions are:

1) Establishing identity and knowledge of children's various cultures and beliefs – fact finding and inclusive approach

2) Looking at self identity and confidence and moving into group identity

Chapter four considers dissonance and conflict, an awareness of difference and racism

The two sessions are:

3) Looking at the challenge in difference: racism and negative stereotyping, power and inequality

4) Conflict resolution: Considering Black role models and people who have fought against discrimination. Examining their character and qualities. Looking at school policies and practices relating to bullying and racism

Chapter six considers creative dissonance, synthesis and transformation of knowledge

The two sessions are:

5) Evaluating learning, stepping back and reflecting on what has been learned from others, integrating different perspectives

6) Recognising dissonance, contrast and creative possibilities. Producing a piece of art

Application

The central aim of all the sessions described through the book is to identify opportunities for collaboration between members of the communities and mainstream teachers to design and deliver curriculum areas together, and to ensure that the children are confident in the classroom to:

■ talk about their cultures and use their own languages

■ evaluate their own and other cultures

■ discuss controversial issues relating to inequality and racism

■ work at solving social and cultural problems and develop new ideas together

Evaluation by the children is essential to understanding what works and why. At the end of the sessions each child should be able to state that:

■ I feel welcome to tell my class about my culture and home lifestyle if I want to

■ I have had a member of my community working in class with my teacher

■ I feel supported if I need to discuss cross-cultural differences and tensions

■ I understand the perspectives of children in my class who come from other backgrounds

■ I know about other cultures in our local community and in the UK

■ I can discuss and evaluate some different cultures and beliefs as well as my own

To develop the learning process as suggested in the lesson plans, activities and materials the at the end of the chapters, the following texts are recommended:

Bowkett, S (1997) *'Imagine That ...' a handbook for creative learning activities in the classroom.* Network Educational Press

Coles, M and Chilvers, P (2003) *Education and Islam: developing a Culturally Inclusive Curriculum.* School Development Support Agency, Leicester City Council. Email: Maurice.coles@dsdsa.net

Commission for Racial Equality (2000) *Learning for All: standards for racial equality in schools* CRE

Origins: *personal stories of crossing the seas to settle in Britain* (1998) Text and video. Published by Origins. The Kuumba Project, Bristol BS2 8UD

Runnymede Trust (2003) *Complementing Teachers: a practical guide to promoting race equality in schools,* (2003). Granada Learning

Ginnis, P (2002). *'The Teachers' Toolkit': raise classroom achievement with strategies for every learner.* Crown House Publishing

Richardson, R (2005) *Here, There and Everywhere: belonging, identity and equality in schools.* Trentham Books in association with Derbyshire Educational Department.

(Richardson's book identifies policies, curriculum, drama and various infrastructures required to support the activities suggested in the chapters in the present book. It also covers themes such as racism, conflict, justice, achievement, and shared humanity and includes inspiring quotes and means of evaluating progress).

Younge, G (1988) *Art of the South African Townships* Thames and Hudson

There is still considerable potential for change through conceptual development: this is not to underestimate the essential political and social changes required but rather to stress the importance of 'opening minds'.

3

The reaffirming response

P2: The younger generation have actually started to realise that ... you know we can be as English as we can but we won't be accepted regardless so why not follow your own religion ... and you'll have an identity at the same time saying 'this is what we are'.

S1: It's just the fact that you immediately belong there [in the Punjab].

B3: I like being a Bangladeshi, I'm proud of it ... I can't just ignore my Bangladeshi people.

Traditional South Asian dress, a clear expression of difference, evokes a sense of controversy and enigma. There is an underlying assumption that people will eventually become assimilated into UK society and this display of difference is dismissed as a temporary phase. Decades later, however, this does not seem to be what is happening. Perhaps most surprisingly, some young women and girls have decided to voluntarily wear the *hijab* (covering, headscarf). Dress is the most conspicuous display of identity; other manifestations relate to practices and values.

South Asian identity and response to living in the UK presents a challenge: its endurance is never completely explained as a temporary phase nor as just a negative response to the pressures adaptation demands. Its tenacity implies that there is something profound and enduring about the beliefs and practices expressed. This conscious display of difference may be puzzling because it can evoke powerfully negative responses from others in society. This chapter aims to explain what is being sustained and why.

The traditional/resistance identity

Castells (1997) as a Spanish academic and sociologist now based in the US identifies a response to the West that can explain some of this display of difference. Castells categorises it as a *resistance* response. This is exemplified by the defiance to maintain what has traditionally held meaning, rather than to adapt. It explains some of what outsiders see as conservative and old-fashioned practices perceived to belong to *traditional* cultures of the past. And on first encounter, what is being said and expressed does appear to endorse the most reactionary interpretations of South Asian traditions. Certain members of the communities emphasised the importance of clear rules, codes of behaviour and respect for authority, as well as an acceptance of certain distinctively non-western features of family life. Bangladeshi spokesperson B1 had this to say:

B1:   Respect everyone; really respect the Elders, especially the Elders because like I said Bengali culture is different [from UK culture].

B1 later gave an example of how an Elder would construe a situation. This example illustrates the authority that an Elder would assume, as well as the clear set of customs and beliefs that order and justify certain behaviours. In this instance it is in relation to a future daughter-in-law:

And my mum [B1's mother would be considered to be an Elder by virtue of her age] came out of the car and she says I've never seen a girl like that in my entire life, just as well we didn't like her; even if we did I'd have said no [to a marriage with her son] – who wants a girl like that; she showed no respect ... My mum was saying that she [the girl's mother] should have told her daughter how to behave ... we'd seen her [the daughter] and then she should have stayed away from the limelight.

B1 appears to be fixed in the past also, impressed by a past that from a western perspective may seem controversial:

B1   I sat next to my gran and ... my gran said I was about the age of your sister when I got married into this family and I was like wow gran you were about five when you got married and she was like yeh I was about five when I got married ... granddad ... he must have been that age as well ... I was like what did you do all day? And she was like I used to play with my dollies (laughs). And that's amazing because that's a story for me to remember all my life and when my child grows up I'll tell him that story you know how my grandma was about five and how she used to play with her dollies. You know if I didn't go to Bangladesh – my gran's dead now – she's been dead for the past five years – I wouldn't have heard these stories.

Such an outlook suggests attitudes towards women that would be unacceptable in the West. B1 also perceived the difference between an English mother and a Bangladeshi mother:

B1:   And a Bengali mother would never say ... 'Oh I have to have a couple of hours off to myself' or 'I have to have a couple of hours away from my baby'. A Bengali mother would never say that. I mean there is not a single parent that would say that. They're there for the child, they'll always be and they'll never say that.

However, people clearly recognised some difference between expectations in Bangladesh and within the UK communities. I shared the content of the letter below with an extended Bangladeshi family in the UK. The letter was a response to an exercise in written English. A young Bangladeshi woman was asked to write a page about what she understood to be the difference for women living in her country and those living in the UK and wrote this (*the grammar has been edited*).

'Dear Sophia sister ... women who live in our country have a sorrowful time. In our society women don't get as much honour as men. Everyone neglects women. Besides this, when a woman gives birth to a daughter she has to turn to her family for their support and sympathy. When the girl grows up, she does not get as much food, clothes and education as a boy. After that, when the girl is sixteen, seventeen or eighteen years old (like me), her father and mother give her in marriage to a boy and the bridegroom's family lots of goods. As a result the girl's education falls into a disturbing position and she gives birth to so many children that this is also a burden to her. She cannot do anything about this because this is her fate as a woman. It is considered to be her fault that she is a woman. In the West women get their full rights. They can do whatever they like, they are not a burden for their family and they are independent ...'

The Bangladeshi families in the UK generally responded to this letter by asserting that though things are changing there is still no real choice. Several members of the communities I showed the letter to found it honest and truthful. They believed that in the UK, women are more independent and equal to men even if they are married. They said that you are not allowed out on your own in Bangladesh but you are here. The eldest daughter of one family and her cousin said that the family could sometimes be a bit of a problem because family members do not always understand what you feel and at times friends can prove to be more understanding. For these two women, friends are as important as family. They recognised that the Bangladeshi mothers are seen to be more like housewives even here, and expected to teach their children about Islam; that women do more work, especially in the home, but that in Bangladesh it is easier for them because they often have servants or relatives help out. Family responsibilities in the UK are intensified for women because as both parents are expected to go out to work there is less time to look after children and it is harder to find child-care.

Contrasting practices and beliefs

The contrast between South Asian and western expectations and experiences of male/female relationships can create tensions. Shaw (1994) quotes a South Asian Pakistani participant's perception of western attitudes to women. 'English women are like toys for men to play with. They are outside, out on the streets, in shops, or on the television. They are cheap and they are for anyone to take'(p53). Shaw argues that Pakistani women's greatest fear is that their men should establish relationships with English women. Any indication of South Asian women behaving like English women will be seen as corrupting the cultural image of women.

There is a perception of the West as less ordered and 'loose' in its conduct, and this was suggested by B1.

B1:   I mean when my son grows up I won't ask ... I want him to have a bit of all that [reference to a certain leniency compared to her parents] but there is a limit on the freedom he will have. I wouldn't let him totally out of my hands like an English mother does when they're sixteen and they are welcome to do whatever they like – no I will have a set of rules for him as well.

This control was seen as essential because, as B1 put it,

I have seen a few Bengali families who you know let their children do what they want and then they can't control these children [and then the children] try to do too much in too short time.

A different appearance, rules, rituals and expectations of belonging can create cross-cultural tensions. From this Bangladeshi perspective parents would feel anxious about letting their children socialise too freely with other children outside school and concerned lest their children pick up unacceptable cultural habits from others in the school. So it appears that this strictness and control emanates partly from a sense of fear about loosing old practices that have value.

This fear of the corrupting influence of the West relates to aspects of globalisa_____ _____ _____ _____ n theories and criti_____ _____ r the existence of _____ n threaten an indivic_____ ocuses on the aspec_____ y. He suggests that _____ sense of anonymit_____ ot create the oppor_____ ciety can thus be se_____ tion and meaning t_____

Alienation _____ created by technol_____ lore the combined _____ hanges. Baudrillard _____ y structures of con_____ lity that perpetuates _____ its hegemonic cont____. Beck (1991) identifies current western society as a *risk* society where there has been a shift in awareness, uncertainty, dependence and trust that has arisen from both technological and conceptual developments. This concept of risk relies on a sense of autonomy and independence to deal strategically with any challenge it presents. A particular cultural mindset is thus foregrounded which may be alien to traditional societies.

For more traditional societies, globalisation and hyperreality can present a profound threat. Giddens (1994) argues that globalisation has alienated traditional communities. He sees globalisation as incorporating the local, personal and intimate elements of life with concepts of time and space that appear to be indefinite. He differentiates between the traditions of the past in terms of formulaic truths and argues that the formulaic truths of the past legitimised traditional power and gave certain members of society the ability to control time. In his view, the present deconstruction of past traditions can create a sense of ontological insecurity in which formulaic truth is antithetical to the process of rational enquiry – where there is no choice but to choose. Giddens explains how globalisation calls for a rational justification of the traditions often simply accepted in some communities.

Castells (1997) identifies a resistance identity that rejects a dominant western culture and identity. It also responds to the way in which values such as Islam are devalued and stigmatised. This response is manifest in a form of enclosure and strengthening of particular communities' non-western values and beliefs, combined with a rejection of globalisation. Castells argues that these devalued communities then react against the denial of their particular cultural ideologies, identities and customs. South Asian communities and religious minority communities within the UK may thus attempt to resist the white, western, secular and, most threateningly, culturally indistinct image that globalisation may appear to have. Rassool (1999) notes that "second generation immigrants' may 'dis-identify with the dominant cultures, as a means of rejecting the culture of those who reject and marginalize them as 'other" (p30). However, rejection alone does not encapsulate the enthusiasm and endurance that people in my study expressed.

Positive cultural affirmation

Indian psychoanalyst Kakar (1996) to some extent explains what may be positively enduring about staying with South Asian values and beliefs. He directs us to the importance of having a personal identity. The personal identity Kakar acknowledges appears to be enhanced by a cultural identity that creates the sense of meaning in life. This is manifest in the expectations of family ties – the commitments but also the security. Kakar argues that despite an initial attempt to become assimilated into western societies, the second generation of South Asians has opted to seek out their origins.

> Many migrants, who have willingly chosen to thoroughly assimilate themselves into their new societies and appear to have lost all traces of their ethnic origins, are surprised to find that the issues of cultural identity have not disappeared. They have only skipped a generation ... sons and daughters ... have become preoccupied with their cultural roots as part of their quest for a personal identity. (p150)

There was clarity and a sense of affirmation in the way people described themselves as 'South Asian'(or specifically as Sikh, Bangladeshi or Pakistani). The evident pride and emotion that was expressed about being South Asian did not touch upon the 'strictness', 'order', sense of difference or more calculated explanations for this affiliation but rather conveyed a sense of spontaneity. In her introductory comments, B1 emphasised:

B1:   As for being Bangladeshi I love it.

B2 was enthusiastic about Bangladeshi cultural activities, still maintained in the UK.

SCG:And you have that lovely poetry session as well.

B2:   Yes every first and third of the month ... and everybody likes to sing as well ... Did you hear Bengalis singing as well?

To maintain an appreciation and knowledge of Bangladeshi lifestyles, the interviewees felt it was essential for their children to visit Bangladesh. B2 emphasised the importance of visits to Bangladesh to refresh cultural knowledge and identity. Bangladeshi parents emphasised that these visits were important to reaffirm the meaning and historical roots of their identity.

B2:   And if you think about holidays, people only go to Bangladesh – that's their holiday ...

SCG: What do you think are the things that are going to sustain the culture?

B2:   Going back to Bangladesh is I think the main thing because otherwise you can't sort of refresh yourself and the kids; their language just becomes stilted in this country. If they go to Bangladesh it'll just revive everything and freshen them up.

B2 expanded upon the cultural features of Bangladesh. She drew attention to the sense of intimacy people in Bangladesh enjoy. She described how people often gather to chat about almost anything.

B2:   Oh they [Bangladeshis] like talking about anything and everything; they love 'addar' it's called. Bangladeshis are famous for...

SCG: What's it called?

B2:   'Udda'...

SCG: Is that chatting?

B2:   It's just chatting – you have meetings with people and you're just chatting the hours away. We did that yesterday; we just popped into somebody's without announcing ... although things are changing as well because people's lives are so busy. People just drop in and say 'hello' ...That's trying to keep all the Bengali traditions – making *slapsa* or what we call snacks. Always wanting people to be here or inviting people over.

The pupils endorsed this enthusiasm for being immersed in Bangladeshi culture. One participant said that it was exciting because you meet more people and can speak another language. Others enthused about the food, games and general experience:

C4(B): And you can walk around with your bare feet and play cricket and football and eat good food and hot spices.

Another added:

C2(B): Especially like the restaurant food, that's nice.

The distinctiveness of ways of life in Bangladesh prompted an awareness of differences across cultures. Even the pupil who had never been to Bangladesh had learnt, from a visiting uncle, about the differences between Bangladesh and the UK.

C3(B): And we, I have, how do you say sasa in um? ... an uncle coming from Bangladesh to here but he didn't know really anything about this place and I had to explain to him.

SCG: What sort of things did you explain?

C3(B): I said you have to learn how to cross the road because in Bangladesh there ain't roads [or pavements] ... And in Bangladesh there are film posters of actresses and actors and I had to explain to him that there ain't any here.

Enthusiasm about the positive contrast between Pakistan and the UK was also indicated by C6 (P) and C9 (P)'s comments:

C6(P): You can walk anywhere you like ... just go wherever you like.

And in another interview:

C9(P): It's cos it's a free country.

These comments can be understood in the light of P1's explanation that parents feel that the people around them in Pakistan have the same values and understanding, so parents can feel relaxed about letting their children wander around.

These pupils clearly felt emotionally and personally proud to have knowledge of Pakistan or Bangladesh and to be linked to their relatives there.

Comments from various pupils reflected the dominance of family ties in the Subcontinent: C2(B) mentioned how much he enjoyed 'Seeing all the relatives I've seen before. Plus when I went to Bangladesh I saw my mum's uncle's wife who died after we came back ... You know Sabia – you know after I came back, after one month my granddad died. And when I went this year it was my auntie's wedding'. However, it was not just about connecting with the family but knowing about the stories that elderly relatives could pass on. C1(B) said 'I was lucky to see my great grandmother ... my grand mum always use to sleep in ... and when I ran past she always used to call to me and she used to talk to me.'C4(B) added: ' and tell you stories' and C1(B) continued 'They tell you all sorts about what happened to your mum and that and what she was like when she was little'.

This identification with a community expressed as an identity conveyed not just a way of living but also something substantial, definable and positively affirming. It affirmed a sense of self-belief, knowledge and skills – skills and knowledge that were passed down through generations and embedded culture with religion. C8(P) emphasised how his grandfather is his role model.

C8(P):   I just like following my religion, following my grandfather because I'm following what my grandfather does.

Religious identity

Children and people felt that religion gave a deeper sense of meaning to their lives. Kakar (1996) argues that religious identities can predominate over other group identities such as class and profession. For instance class and profession can appear to lack an encompassing world-view and are impoverished in terms of symbolic riches and so comparatively meaningless. The interviewees affirmed the importance of their religious texts in terms of the meaning for their lives.

B2:   They [children] need to read Arabic so that they can read the Koran because once you can read the Koran you'll be able to learn the verses that you need to know for *namas* [prayers]. And then there's the sort of background about how we do certain customs. So that's how my dad sort of did it with me. He did read stories of the prophets and what they did and that gives a background and meaning to your life.

SCG: So what do you think are most important in a child's education?

B3:   I think they should know about Islam.

SCG: That's the most important?

B3:   That's the most important thing for Muslim people – like my children go to school, but every evening I take them to the Mosque. Every Monday, Tuesday and Friday.

Islam was clearly the most powerful and reaffirming element of this group's identity. It united them with other Muslims in the local communities and in the world.

SCG: What's it like to be a Muslim?

B3 I also feel good to be a Muslim and proud to be a Muslim.

SCG: Do you think that's quite different from being Bangladeshi?

B3: Yeh Bangladeshi – it's just a country – like Pakistani it's just the name – like this is England, ... just [a] name ... [whereas being] Muslim – we all are like Pakistani people; so many people are Muslim – they have to pray all the time five times a day; you're born to be Muslim.

SCG: What do you think is the most important thing?

B3: Remember God. And if you don't remember God there are things you have to do ... I have to follow Islam.

South Asian children also emphasised the meaningfulness of their religious identity and knowledge.

C5(B): The Mosque is the most important [as compared with school] ... Cos you get to go – when you die you get to go to heaven ... Yeh so that means we're praying to go to heaven ...

C3(B): In the first time when you finish the Koran or *Sufara* or *Hyda* you have to give out food – that's what we call *Shinli*.

Great status was attached to going to Mecca: 'Oh it's beautiful' was the response of one pupil C6 (P) who had made the pilgrimage.

It seemed clear from such comments that the pupils understood others, including the school, through their understanding of life as conveyed through their religious upbringing. Learning about prayer involved the whole family.

C9 (P): Like I do it at home and my dad he has to learn it all.

Prayer books were accorded particular respect.

C8(P): The difference between this school and the Mosque as well is that if you lose the books you have to pay one pound to get a new one or something. So that's like gold.

C9(P): Five pounds for losing the Koran and if you get it back you have to kiss it.

C7(P): It's like sent from Allah to Mohammed.

Although enthusiasm and belief were powerful forces for adhering to religious practices, rules and authoritarian practices could be identified that enforced commitment. Fear of the *Shitan* [devil] and respect for Allah made rules and tests in life meaningful so school and Mosque were seen in parallel: 'It's like tests – like the Shitan making ... Like the Shitan and Allah. So they've got these competitions. How much people go to heaven ... It depends if they're a good or bad person.'

Religious tests for life meant being good, working hard and to please God – apparently a powerful incentive for the pupils:

C7(P): It's a good deed, like it's hard work to be a Muslim, it's really, really hard; I reckon it's the hardest religion to have to be five times a day. You have to go to school, go to the Mosque, you have a really long day and a really long week.

SCG: So why do you do all this?

C9(P): Because we do it to please our God.

C7(P): Allah.

C8(P): This is not a real life really; Allah is seeing if – whether we're proper Muslims or if we're not then I don't know what happens.

C7(P): This life is a practice – it's like Allah just likes seeing if you're good in this life and then sending you to heaven or hell. It's so that you can learn it for when you get older and when you go to *Hadj* you can know what to wear and things like that.

C8(P): It's proud to be a Muslim and it's a good deed, and if you do something wrong you can be forgiven because you can go to the Mosque.

Furthermore this sense of being 'good' was seen to connect closely to what your parents, and not just the Mosque, believed. Religious beliefs were closely aligned to a way of life and meaning for the family. The pupils wove their religious and family beliefs together.

C2(B): Cos like if you're like a Muslim, Allah gives you clues to life. It says in the Koran yeh – always listen to your mum. It's like for example if like you say can you go to football practice to your mum and your mum goes 'no' – like this happened last time. I said can I go to the park and play ... cricket. And my mum said 'no' and I crept there anyway and there was another cricket team there already and the day after the cricket match my mum said 'yeh I told you always listen to your mum or what you want won't come true'.

Thus religion served to reinforce respect for the rules and order in the family. It was considered foolish to ignore rules:

C1(B): You listen to your parents [or] you get lost yeh and you get kidnapped and your parents won't even know.

The pupils emphasised the certainty, order and meaning that Islam brought to their lives:

C1(B): If you are a believer you go to the Mosque or Church – we read the Koran because when we die Allah's going to ask us questions and some of the questions, like the answers will be in the Koran.

C2(B): If you're a good Muslim then Allah's going to like make you speak.

This was contrasted with the apparent lack of meaning or clarity associated with being a non-believer, which the pupils did not relish:

C4(B): If you're a Muslim then you have to do some special things and if you're just like a normal person then you just do what you want.

C1(B): Some people are non-believers.

C2(B): Don't believe in anything.

SCG: What do you think about non-believers?

C2(B): They can do anything they want ...

C1(B): But we don't want to believe in [just] anything; we want to believe in Allah.

Belief in Allah echoed through family meanings and dominated cultural practices.

Kakar (1996) identifies how religious beliefs and practices emanate from a deep inner sense of personal and communal identification with a particular set of beliefs and practices. He emphasises that '[primordiality] related to shared myths, memories, values and symbols ... assumes a vital healing function, shared idealism ... ties of loyalty ... intense moments ... feelings of fusion and merger' (p149). Modood (1994) and Ballard (1994) have registered the importance of this identity within the corpus of South Asian identities.

Combining cultural, religious and familial meanings

Although religion may well be the most powerful element in people's lives, incorporating practices, written scripts, languages and meanings that exist across the world and produce a 'brotherhood' or 'sisterhood' of connection, its influence cannot be separated from cultural and familial/communal elements. Religion, culture and the family are entwined to create a dynamic web of possible answers to the problems created by living in the UK. When one answer proved too rigid another was sought for refuge. For instance, when marriages were too difficult Islam presented a way out: divorce was acceptable even if the culture and family resist change of this nature. Similarly when an edict from the Mosque appeared too rigid, for instance when singing and music were deemed threatening because they evoked sensual temptations that might lure a person away from their devotion, culture presented another perspective. All those who had been to Bangladesh expressed excitement about the cultural festivities they had seen. The conversation below illustrates how families, cultural traditions and religion are enmeshed:

C1(B): Miss did you see the people dancing in Bangladesh? ...

C2(B): Yes ... they [musicians] come to your house and they start playing music.

SCG: For a religious reason or just?

C2(B): No just singing.

SCG: It's a Bangladeshi tradition?

C1(B): But they are Muslims.

C1(B): Yeh all my family ... my grandma and grandpa were dancing!

C4(B): And one time when you have to stay in the Mosque all night it happens – like two times a year.

C1(B): We're just lucky.

C4(B): We're just lucky cos I went in the wintertime and it happens in the winter so I went there.

Giddens (1994) argues that rituals are functional, providing a sense of emotional autonomy for the reflexive projection of the self. The combination of belief, enthusiasm and rationalisation for reaffirming South Asian identity and a response to the wider UK culture provides a deep emotional and ontological security. South Asian identities are multifaceted, with a powerful religious aspect which may overarch the others and create a strong sense of collectivity.

Despite this sense of collectivity there were incompatibilities. Differences as well as similarities existed between the different cultural groups; between the responses within each community and between the generations.

Differences have the potential to create conflicts between Pakistani, Sikh and Bangladeshi groups. For instance, Conway and Haque (1999), in their study of autobiographical memory, note the profound effect the 1971 war between Pakistan and Bangladesh has had on Bangladeshis.

Different responses also exist within each community, and even within families, over the degree of conformity and their response to general values and beliefs.

B2:   Some people who are very strict would say that singing is against religion, but I don't take that on board. I feel that's our leisure time and it enhances us. We wouldn't be able to do poems if people were like that but ... I think it's the fanatics and the Mullahs who try to control people and who are not very educated themselves; they believe those things. They use it as a way of controlling people.

Diversity and difference

This flexibility and diversity within the general expression of a re-affirming response may also change in different contexts. When there is an assumption that the people you are with share the same view as you or have the same loyalties, it is safer to be critical about the limitations of one's cultural group or identity. Similarly if a person is in their home and not sitting in their community building representing their culture and community, they are likely to feel under less pressure to act as a spokesperson.

Different positions within family structures can influence different experiences of western culture and different linguistic knowledge. This is most conspicuous between Elders and younger members of the communities.

There was no unanimous, unequivocal perspective on the responses to the challenges presented. Furthermore, intergenerational communication could promote change. Perspectives on the issues that arose varied. Nearly all the interviewees felt that their community had itself adapted and changed. In the communities there was a definite sense of change, reflection and movement. B1 noted the positive way things had changed for young Bangladeshis living in the UK:

B1:   It is easier now, much easier. I mean my mum used to go there in her sari, you know her bright sari and I used to see her a mile off ... It used to be embarrassing ... I'll let her [her daughter] wear long skirts, I'll let her wear shirts with long sleeves, I'll let her wear trousers – I won't nag at her ... things are changing.

Khan (1992) notes how even in the 1990s South Asian women were already adapting their designs, adjusting to different influences: 'Walk down any street in a so-called 'Asian area' and you can see the range of allegiances now presented: saris and home-made shalwar, designers' suits and jeans. Mobility and choice are far greater than even ten years ago' (p73-4).

The greatest hopes of change were expressed by B3, who had felt under pressure to remarry. B3 'They [people in the community] even say get married don't waste your life.' Her position as a divorcee had made her happier socialising in other South Asian groups, such as at Pakistani and Sikh community gatherings. Nonetheless at the end of two years she talked of change:

B3:   [The community] is changing in that it's not just like the back-
        ground – like the way things were before – like mostly arranged
        marriages were done but now like so many people think about
        love marriage or to see the person they are going to marry and –
        I feel like less force.

The concept of 'love marriages' shows the influence of western culture. The prevalence of 'other' beliefs demands a more complex and reflective response to living in the UK. Religious belief itself represents a definite schism with many western identities where religion has been rejected. This schism also represents a fundamental difference from others in the UK. This assertion of 'other beliefs' as substantiated by family rules and practices does not encapsulate the more evaluative responses to being Muslim or South Asian in the UK. Gidden's belief that traditional societies just accept the past does not capture the challenge expressed by those 'other' non western belief systems in the UK. A solution to the cross-cultural tensions could be identified as a critical understanding of the experiences among the various members of the communities. This critical understanding brought elements of the various South Asian communities together, and influenced them to be more confident of their divergence from western values in general. S1 was suspicious of the seemingly boundless sense of freedom that she felt the West promotes:

S1:   Freedom is so – I think that probably why so many Indians come
        across here [is] because they think it's going to be so free. But it's
        not until they realise that it's not so free ... freedom was [when
        she was a teenager], it was something luring you that way ...
        temptation isn't it?

This critique of a secular society, which appears decadent and illusory, may look like a rejection of the West rather than a positive assertion of difference. But again it is the enthusiasm and assertion of something qualitatively different that provides sustenance and peace. This qualitative dimension as manifest in clearly different set of beliefs and values is understood through Armstrong's (2000) identification of *mythos*.

In her profound analysis of Islam, Christianity and Judaism, Karen Armstrong (2000) identifies the roots to the possible misunder-standings that can occur between secular and non-secular world-views and reveals the incompatibilities between the two. She des-cribes how religious identity is closely tied to a whole cultural world that reflects not only particular beliefs but rather a belief in beliefs. Myths and legends, too, become part of the meaning in life. She identifies the difference between a spiritual meaning in life and the pragmatic rationalism of the West. She describes the difference be-tween *logos* and *mythos*, both of which were regarded as indis-pensable in the pre-modern world. She observes that because modernisation is based purely upon logos (or rational arguments) it can discount *mythos* as false and superstitious. However, logos can-not answer questions about the ultimate value of human life, the meaning of life. *Mythos* (myth and cult) is concerned less with what actually happens and more with the meaning of an event. The modern world is seen as future-orientated and able, for tech-nological as well as philosophical reasons, to ignore the past and myths. For those religions and cultures that still recognise the im-portance of *mythos*, 'modernisation is often experienced not as a liberation but as an aggressive assault' (pxvi).

Belief in beliefs

There were intriguing instances when a *belief in beliefs* combined with a cultural fable or story appeared to synthesise and affirm identity. The extended family in Bangladesh was a great resource in terms of 'stories'. These stories also embodied a mixture of myth and fantasy. Most importantly, they were entwined with the meanings that old cultures maintain through stories in the same way fairy stories originating in the mountainous forests of Germany, such as *Hansel and Gretel,* act to warn children away from venturing into the forest. So Bangladeshi myths in a country that suffers from tidal waves and flooding dwelt on the dangers of water and the sea. The following interview with the pupils captures a sense of mystery and imagination. It was evident that community and home life cir-culated beliefs originating in the Subcontinent. We see their sense of pride in their identities and identification based upon these shared stories and mysteries:

C1(B): Miss do you know there's mermaids in Bangladesh?

C2(B): Yeh bad mermaids.

SCG: Bad mermaids – what do the bad mermaids do?

C2(B): They pull you under water then they ...

C1(B): No when you're swimming like they pull your legs half way and you're going to start drowning and then you've got to kick them off; you've got to kick them hard.

C2(B): There's a kind of monster at the corner of the swimming pool.

C1(B): And he just grabs you and pulls you underwater.

SCG: Do you believe that?

C1(B): I don't know.

C4(B): You never know it might be true!

C1(B): My grandfather he died, miss he died in the swimming pool.

C2(B): I do believe in ghosts.

The stories had obviously captured the children's imagination and they expressed a sense of the awe and mystery they wished to preserve. Possibly too, their sense of belief gathered through the religious element in their lives made these stories or myths more believable. There was clearly a link between the myths surrounding Bangladesh and the stories told by Imams in the Mosque:

C4(B): At the end [of a session in the Mosque] sometimes they [the imams] tell you stories ...

SCG: What sort of stories do they tell you?

C4(B): About the prophets.

C2(B): And about the ghosts.

Abu-Lughod (1986) describes how poetry is closely woven into the personal life, meanings and beliefs for cultures that draw upon an Arabic tradition. For such religions and cultures the western atheistic and secular world may by contrast appear predominantly cynical and meaningless. The alternative life that drew culture, religion and family together could claim greater resonance and meaning. Combining art with religion raises experience to a level of transcendence, beyond the mundane.

So it was not just the sometimes, constraining, concrete rules, rituals and places that were crucial to this religious identity and meaning. Paradoxically, the spiritual space that existed for those who believed provided openness through the mystery that spiritualism creates. S2 emphasised the importance of a spiritual existence and space in life.

S2:   I keep the tape on – I listen to the *Gurbani* [Sikh hymns and prayers] tape every morning and that kind of gives you a sense of peace within and in your household ... my mother-in-law has a little room in which she keeps the Guru Granthsab which is a place of worship and like she'll try and teach our kids that as soon as they come in they must go and bow to that. So they know it's in the house and acknowledge that space.

When S2 was asked: 'What makes them Sikh do you think?' She replied, 'What's within ... '

In this way the sacred space for contemplation was highly respected. Religious belief and practice interwoven with cultural meanings and diverse interpretations offered a greater range of possibilities than may at first be apparent to an outsider. However, there was one more crucial layer beneath the layers of belief, practices, even identities that appeared to lie at the heart of an affirming response to having a South Asian identity.

The Heartland

South Asian identity conveys not just an assertion of difference and a commitment to another way of life and understanding; it represents something that affirms you. It gives you recognition, affiliation with others and a deep sense of ownership. You are no longer an immigrant or an outsider but someone who is welcome and belongs. S1, the Sikh spokesperson and P3, the Pakistani radical also voiced a deep attachment to their cultural identity and connection with their land of origin, even though P3 had never been there:

S1 expressed a profound sense of belonging: 'It's just the fact that you immediately belong there.'

The sense that the wider UK society does not identify with you, nor accept your different values and beliefs, intensifies the feeling of being accepted by your land of origin. P3 for example feels that only in Pakistan will the meaning of her life be properly respected and will she feel happy to ultimately rest:

P3:   If I was going to die I'd rather get buried over there than over here ... I would hate ... to be buried here and no one goes to your grave ... out there you are with your own kind.

The most important and positive aspect of identifying oneself as South Asian seemed to be that you belong, and that there is a world, a physical place that you could call your home, even if it is on the other side of the world. This place would welcome you and affirm your being – it would want you to be part of it. It was a place in which you could trust.

C6(P): All of us three we spend most of our life in England but we're Muslims really ...

C7(P): We've got Pakistani families and Pakistani ancestors ... My name is ... I am a Muslim and I'm born in [the locality in this study] and I am proud to be a Muslim and I see myself as a British citizen but I'd put Pakistani first.

Participants were eager to expand upon their experiences and family connections in Bangladesh: *their* country. It was noticeable that they expressed their home of origin and its features in the first person possessive. For instance one pupil stated:

C2(B): I like going there because I can visit all my relatives and ... [it's] *my own* country (author's emphasis).

One child who had never visited expressed great excitement about the possibility.

With this sense of ownership came pride in what went on in their country.

South Asian religious, cultural and social practices are thus held within a powerful emotional belief that you are a valuable being: that you belong. This sense of belonging engenders a sense of well-being which is self affirming as much as it affirms the beliefs and values themselves: as a Bangladeshi Muslim, for example, the sense of self belongs within a body of practices and beliefs. This different way of experiencing life in the UK and attachment to the Sub-continent can remind us, as human beings, that some of the most fundamental aspects of our own lives; our sense of belonging, positive identity and self belief can be engendered through cultural beliefs and practices.

The reaffirming response appeared to encapsulate plurality where difference is accepted apparently without tensions. The concept of difference suggests diversity, which can be non-problematic: 'The cultural politics of difference recognises both the interdependent and relational nature of identities, their elements of incommensurability and their political right of autonomy' (Rutherford: 1990: 10).

An affirming South Asian response embeds its cultural meanings and even sense of self within a non-western culture and the West is viewed from this vantage point. In order to protect their South Asian cultural identity and beliefs, certain interviewees described how they avoided situations where their beliefs and practices were challenged: they chose to develop and maintain social centres where their values and beliefs were respected and practised.

Affirmation may be central to understanding the complex exchange, which blend our inner and outer existence, but this ferment may not endure when the outer world encroaches as we step out of the bond that links us. Stepping into the wider society from the enclave of a South Asian community, which the younger generation must do for schooling or job-hunting, presents different challenges. B3 for instance, recognised that community pressure that ignored the perspectives and experiences of young people could ostracise them and influence them to leave it.

SCG: I just wonder how much they [young people] do cope sometimes? You've had all those things to deal with. Can you understand why young people might break away from the community?

B3: Because people in the community don't respect you.

There maybe tensions between the generations due to their different experiences of the wider society. Lack of awareness and discussion within the communities about the cross-cultural dilemmas young South Asians may experience can make it difficult for the younger generation to affirm a South Asian identity or to accept being *different*.

Those young people and families living in the UK who affirm their South Asian identity and also discuss their different perspectives and experiences are more likely to resolve some of the problems that might arise. People expressing this response would also desire schools to show much greater understanding of South Asian religious beliefs and values. Parents would ideally like their children to go to schools that promote their own faith or else another faith, rather than secular beliefs.

Having different priorities and feeling different can make the wider society less alluring. Nonetheless this affirmation of difference can also be a form of avoidance as engagement with the wider society can be avoided. One instance where it becomes inescapable is in relation to school. But the knowledge base of different cultures can be incompatible.

Schools can certainly acquire some knowledge of South Asian culture and integrate some of the different perspectives. Schools can also offer their pupils a sense of belonging. An affirming response focuses upon definition or clarification of cultural values, beliefs and meanings. However, as Chatterjee (1997) argues, these meanings have to be more clearly adapted so that change and modernisation are not just western concepts. And they have to be identified before attempting to adapt or change them.

Classroom sessions and activities to foster the reaffirming response

The reaffirming response celebrates diversity and values the sense of belonging which home and communities can offer. It considers the meanings behind some of these beliefs, rituals and practices that may exist locally. It embeds a sense of self within a social context. Who we are, our priorities and sense of belonging need to be understood and established. Sessions are explorative and aim to gather the class's range of personal and social information to analyse and evaluate.

The guidelines for teachers offered below are best followed in collaboration with members of the local communities, a member of staff or an ethnic minority parent. If the teacher and a member from the local communities lead the sessions, this will model diversity from the start.

Key aims of Sessions 1 and 2:

- to encourage curiosity about and interest in other perspectives and experiences
- to explore the diverse beliefs, experiences and cultures in the local communities
- to understand how this exploration is best approached: what questions to ask and how
- to consider and evaluate personal identity
- to question what it means to have a specific cultural identity and how it may link to our personal identity

It important to establish a code of conduct in the sessions so that children feel secure and confident to talk about their personal identity and explore their cultural heritage. The teacher needs to make sure that the children feel a sense of ownership of the sessions and the children, teacher and representative need to pool together a list of rules for each session.

Suggestion for how to present the session:

Over the next six weeks we will be looking at our cultural and social identities including: African, African Caribbean, Mixed Heritage, Irish, Welsh, Scottish, English and Asian people. We shall consider the contributions of other cultures and beliefs to British culture: all your contributions, concerns and interests are welcome. Although a member of staff will be working with you this is *your* group. So you can make the decisions about the ground rules. These sessions will draw on knowledge from your homes and communities so that the school is better informed and aware.

Rationale underlying ground rules:

- bonding and building rapport
- giving the young people credibility
- teachers (facilitators) divulging their own experience, identity and at times engaging in role play to play an equal part in the sessions.
- stating clearly how learning is best achieved
- ensuring that there is a secure and safe setting in the classroom where cultural beliefs and values can be discovered and discussed.

Teachers need to take care not to defend the school if the children say something negative about it.

At the end of sessions identify what has been achieved and what the next session will be about.

So ground rules may be:

- No rude words
- Don't laugh at other people
- Confidentiality: when private or personal things are said they stay in this room
- No physical violence
- No racist comments/remarks
- Don't ask upsetting questions
- Be kind and respectful
- Don't talk when others are talking

This chapter has drawn on the communities' knowledge, personal identity and belonging with others. Accordingly, the sessions are concerned with:

- establishing identity and knowledge of children's various

cultures and beliefs – fact finding and inclusive approach

■ looking at self identity and confidence and moving into group identity

Session 1 focuses on interviewing skills, fact-finding and discovery.

The pupils consider what their priorities are, what they believe in and what they know about their cultures. They are invited to interview each other in pairs and to interview their parents and families for homework. This interviewing process is discussed to guide the children on how to phrase questions.

Suggested questions to ask in the interviews:

Tell me about your culture/what languages do you speak ...

What happened to you in your childhood that mattered to you?

What makes you feel good?

What is your usual day like – what happens?

Tell me about your cultural background

The resulting ideas, which the pupils share in pairs, are collated and discussed. Then in the second session information brought to class from homes or communities is included and discussed in small groups.

The knowledge obtained can be used to set up the following activities for the class. Teachers may need to ask the class to do a little more specific research to gather the material required.

■ Plan-a-Journey: visit three countries and describe three things about each; describe one spectacular scene and offer one piece of wisdom from a person you met

■ The Alpha Team: children go on a dangerous mission – what will they need – what do they need to know – eg in a flooded area of Bangladesh

■ Or having looked at how people live in another country, what would you need to tell someone visiting from there about family life in Britain

Alternatively:

■ Plan a session with a member of the local communities which draws upon cultural knowledge as suggested in the *Kaamyaabi* sessions outlined in chapter seven. The meanings and beliefs can then be discussed more fully.

■ The teacher and member of the local community study the

contributions various cultures have made to our knowledge, eg that Muslim/Arabic cultures developed mathematical thinking, and integrates this knowledge into a relevant curriculum session (as suggested in chapter seven).

■ The class uses the cultural knowledge they have gained from their research and discussion to design a quiz, and tests the teacher about facts and understanding.

■ Should children be going to India, Pakistan, Somalia or elsewhere before this session, the class should consider what they want to know about the country so that the travellers can gather the information. Give them a copy of *My journey to ...* – the KS1 and KS2 workbooks for children to take abroad, published by Education Bradford. Then when the children return, give them an opportunity to tell the class about what they did and discovered while away.

Session 2 looks at personal identity and group identity. It is also about confidence building which links into the strengths and insights required to be effective (see session five).

Link from the first session: 'Last week was all about our cultures, histories, beliefs etc. Has anyone asked their parents or community members about their values and beliefs? ... This week is about us as individuals; how we feel and think about our lives and others, and about understanding who we are, how others see us and how we see ourselves; what we share and how we differ.'

Key aims of Session 2:

■ understanding what influences how we see ourselves and others

■ identifying how the children see themselves (possibly through symbols/pictures/portrait activity)

■ reflecting upon links in the group

■ valuing each other

■ considering differences and similarities in the group (discussion in pairs for feedback to main group).

Activities:

■ Children fill in circles on a 'this is me' sheet (an A4 sheet with a face in the centre to fill in, surrounded by empty circles to fill with comment

- In pairs pupils take turns to ask each other to identify three good things the other child sees in them
- They write down these good things and start on a self portrait

As a class everyone can share what they have learned about themselves and then discuss what they have in common. This can be followed by a class activity: 'sharing safe havens'. The process for creating a safe haven is set out in *Imagine That*... This activity draws upon children's ability to concentrate on the moment, to listen, and feel dimensions about where they are and then to imagine their ideal space and finally view it from another perspective. This experience can then be shared as a group activity.

The session concludes by identifying how we differ. This sense of difference can lead into the third and fourth sessions (see chapter four).

Other resources

Taken from *Here, There and Everywhere* ... (Richardson, 2005)

Discussing the three philosophical principles Belonging, Identity, Equality (p.5). Citizenship: Discriminating between fact and opinion, looking at media analysis and different perspectives on recent events. Performing Benjamin Zephaniah's poems in *We are Britain*

Design Technology: looking at clothes, food etc around the world

Science: looking at the sources and spread of scientific knowledge

Taken from Complementing Teachers (Runnymede Trust, 2000)

The majority of these links to Key stages 1 and 2 are based in fact finding and awareness of diversity without requiring analysis or elaboration. Older children could explore issues further through games or quizzes that engage them in comparing, contrasting, evaluating and applying the knowledge gathered.

Citizenship: Myself in the community KS1

Design Technology: Fruit and vegetables around the world

English: Bilingual texts of stories KS1; Stories from other cultures KS1 + 2 The Fox and the Crocodile – a traditional story from Bangladesh KS2

Geography: Our local area KS1; Global Climates KS2 and; What's in the news (adapted from QCA unit)

ICT: Me and My Things KS1; Talking about Friendship, Equality, Diversity and Community using a Roamer KS2

Mathematics: Reasoning and generalising about Numbers – introducing numerals in different cultures KS2; Equivalent Fractions – exploring the Islamic law of Inheritance KS4

Physical Education: Bhangra Dance KS2

Personal Social and Health Education: The family KS2

Religious Education: Our local community KS1; Healers KS2

Science: Food and Healthy Eating KS2; Kites (Kite flying is a national sport in the Punjab) KS3;

Visual and Three-Dimensional Art: Self Portrait KS1; Investigating Pattern KS2

Conclusion

The responses recorded in this chapter register difference as a positive decision to celebrate and enjoy having a clear sense of belonging, identity and cultural knowledge. Children's socio-cognitive skills are exercised when they compare and contrast. Considering contrasting knowledge and beliefs is further explored in the next chapter. There are also implicit challenges in identifying difference. In their engagement with the wider society, whether through school or work, members of South Asian communities may experience tensions and disjunctures that have somehow to be addressed. Facing disjuncture and feeling like an outsider can manifest in contradictory and constrained responses, which express disorientation, dissonance and some confusion. They are central to the cross-cultural predicament, as we shall see.

4
The contradictory and compromised response

B2: I find it a bit difficult to mix at times ... you feel like an outcast ... And I suddenly realise, that they were treating me with kid gloves sort of thing ... people ask if I'd like a drink or go to the pub; because they know I'm a Muslim that question doesn't always come – but you don't want them to ignore you. You do want them to ask you to come down to the pub because other-wise you feel an outcast.

P2: It's very difficult trying to keep your identity these days because there are so many influences out there ... I mean I couldn't cope with our religion but you just have to ...

This contradictory response reflects the pressures and tensions experienced by South Asian communities living in western society. It shows their conspicuous desire to mix in wider society and resolve tensions but also the lack of support and aware-ness in wider society and schools. The previous chapter outlined differences between the participants' values and beliefs and those in wider society. These differences can create tensions in relation to education, religion, expectations of family and community life, and affect the sense of self. The sense of difference becomes a problem of disjuncture; it is no longer about just being aware but rather about attempts at engagement and the consequences.

Disjuncture
Disjuncture implies tension, unease, discomfort and conflict, the subordination and unequal position of a person or a community.

This disjuncture exists for many communities, such as New Age Travellers or African Caribbean communities. Blackledge (2000) and Vincent (2001) identify the way in which South Asian voices in particular are silenced and omitted from the school agenda. Issues of immigration, imperialism, colonialism (see Said, 1993; 1997; Chatterjee, 1997) and globalisation (Castells, 1997) all put the South Asian communities in a subordinate position.

An important distinction between disjunction and difference relates to external views of the South Asian community and also to their views of themselves and their consequent responses to wider society. Disjuncture occurs at a point of potential juncture, where there is a need to interact and integrate but integration is impeded, so producing incompatibilities, incoherence and conflict. A lack of exchange indicates not only a conflict of identification but also disjuncture of purpose and ideology. Recognising disjuncture also means recognising structural constraints that inhibit individual agency. This may be at a perceptual level and not just a structural level. Vincent (1996) suggests that differences are important because they evoke different expectations that are not reconcilable unless they are recognised. For instance, although educational literature talks of 'the' community outside the school, there is no such homogenous community outside the school. There are instead a variety of communities that believe and behave differently and who do not see themselves as one homogenous community. This disjuncture is due to a misconception about what exists and, most importantly, how others see themselves. Vincent's use of the word difference here indicates the existence of disjuncture.

Disjuncture may occur at an intrapersonal level, where one identity threatens to crush or undermine another. If, say, a woman is both a mother and a teacher, she may feel troubled about neglecting her mother identity and the expectations surrounding it because of the time and energy her teacher role and identity takes up. A Muslim may feel happy to mix with people of other faiths and cultures within a community, so just operating with difference – until she is required to subjugate her faith to other practices. Then disjuncture may occur, perhaps when the *Azan* (call to prayer) is not recognised as important within daily routines at work or school. Challenges such as these may occur at perceptual and not just circumstantial level. Recognising disjuncture brings the problems of resolving the discontinuities, so Muslims in this situation may have to withhold or repress their beliefs consciously or subconsciously, to remain conciliatory.

The communities demonstrated different degrees of engagement with UK society. Some avoided it, as we have seen, but in relation to education this is not an option. Others did want to integrate more but not at the cost of losing their sense of cultural identity, values and beliefs. Although this shows a movement towards greater integration, it at the same time captures a sense of tension. Problems and difficulties are more pronounced than in the re-affirming response. Difficulties are experienced at various levels due to fundamental differences and structural disadvantages relating to racism and prejudice in society. Differences between cultural expectations about the meaning of education, the appropriateness of the school curriculum and the teachings in the Mosques can create confusion. Misunderstandings appear to stem from a lack of communication as well as a lack of knowledge of all concerned. These confusions and misunderstandings create psychological problems.

Kakar (1996) points to the pain caused by being marginalised, misunderstood and dehumanised by bureaucratic structures. 'Cultural identity, like its individual counterpart, is an unconscious human requirement which becomes consciously salient only when there is a perceived threat to its integrity' (p 150). Kakar's insight suggests a reactionary state of bereavement and in this context a negative reaction to what threatens the maintenance of non-western practices is inevitable.

The interaction between fear of loosing one's culture at a personal and social level is exacerbated by the way in which the host culture responds. Ghuman (1999) notes how the zeitgeist and reception from the wider society can affect the response of the immigrant: 'The decision to integrate does not entirely rest on the immigrants and their descendents but also – perhaps more so – on the reaction of the host culture' (p25). And in his study of imperialism, Said (1993) points to the excluding nature of large cultural groups so that 'Culture comes to be associated, often aggressively, with nation or state; this differentiates 'us' from 'them' ... Culture in this sense is a source of identity ... Culture in this way can become a protective enclosure' (pxii-xv). Thus larger cultures dismiss or deride certain identities.

The background to experience of this kind and the consequent response is less easily identified in literature. It may be the more transitory and elusive response but it none the less captures some of the struggle entailed in trying to move across cultural divides. At its worst, the response to pressures at various levels can be self- rejection, alienation and even suicide. To understand this disturbance it is vital to recognise that the wider society can place severe judgements upon people whom they see as different and impose values and beliefs that are not sensitively adapted to take account of other cultural and historical backgrounds.

The responses in the previous chapter all focused on how identity is formed by affiliation with or rejection of other groups. But identity can also be imposed.

Imposed identity

An imposed identity is unlikely to fit with a person's own views of their identity. Hall directs us to Fanon's (1990) complex analysis of the effect of imposed identity, when he analyses the dismembering of colonised cultures by the colonisers. He shows two different ways of thinking about cultural identity in the context of colonisation: either obliterating it by the colonisers or reclaiming it by the colonised. Fanon describes the nostalgic search for identity among colonised people:

> Passionate research ... directed by the secret hope of discovering beyond the misery of today, beyond self contempt, resignation and abjuration, some very beautiful and splendid era whose existence rehabilitates us both in regard to ourselves and in regard to others. (p169)

Fanon considers that 'Colonisation ... turns the past of oppressed people, and distorts, disfigures and destroys it.'(p169)

Said (1997) exposes the way that the West perpetuates a view of Islam as a monolithic, fundamentalist power and points to the misunderstanding that arises out of this misconception of Islam:

> 'Islam' defines a relatively small proportion of what actually takes place in the Islamic world, which numbers a billion people ... an infinite number of different experiences ... Aside from the combination of hostility and reductionism offered by these misinterpretations, there is the matter of how grossly they exaggerate and inflate Muslim extremism within the Muslim world ... [In the politics of dispossession] I attempted to show how it was secularism, rather than fundamentalism, that held the Arab Muslim communities together ... he [referring to Lewis, a senior British orientalist] simply cannot deal with the diversity of Muslim ... life because it is closed to him as something foreign, radically different, and other.(pxxvi – xxxi)

A key point made by Hall (1990) and Said (1997) is that identity in various ways relates to how others see us, rather than encapsulating a cultural identity that is produced within a community. One factor identified in the literature is how a country views cultural groups who have immigrated there.

This dilemma is voiced clearly by P1 when she articulates the problems that exist for parents and communities living in a UK context rather than on the Subcontinent:

P1:   Out there [in Pakistan] everybody out there is the same and people are thinking in the same way as you, whereas here in our community I may be thinking totally differently from the way the rest of the community is thinking.

There is another dimension to the way in which 'others' can be perceived. Said (1997) describes how western hostility towards Islam is actually a way in which the West creates a sense of its own importance. The *other* is thus distinctly embodied in Islamic beliefs, practices and orientalist perspectives. Said has voiced concern that the western media portrays Islam as a conglomerate mass hostile to the West:

My concern, though, is that the mere use of the label 'Islam' either to explain or indiscriminately condemn 'Islam', actually ends up becoming a form of attack, which in turn provokes more hostility between self-appointed Muslims and the Western spokespersons. (1997: xvi)

Hall (1990) and Fanon (1990) suggest the *other* relates not just to Islam but also to Black cultures and their non-European roots. Communities can be marked by outsiders as different and homogenous and this can affect the insider's view of self as an excluded person or group. Islamophobia is manifest in stereotypical views of Muslims and a belief that the West is implacably hostile to the non-Islamic world, coupled with a belief that the Islamic faith is adhered to for political or military advantage (Conway, 1997).

Other aspects of difference between communities include different languages and histories. Through the process of assimilation the majority frequently impose their own language and devalorise, stigmatise and even eradicate other languages (Hamers and Blanc, 1989). As Said and Hall argue, *different* identities struggle to maintain their particular values and beliefs to sustain specific cultural identities. The concept of speaking a minority language or being part of a minority community is in itself a kind of imposed identity. Working with researchers from other countries Morgan and Joy

(1999) recognise the culturally bounded nature of language, which may inhibit communication.

In the introductory chapter to his collection of essays on identity, Rutherford (1990) explains that in the modern world:

> In the commodification of language and culture, objects and images are torn free of their original referents and their meanings become a spectacle open to almost infinite translation ...The power relation is closer to tourism than imperialism, an expropriation of meaning rather than materials. (p11)

This implies that non-western identities have still to assert their own meanings so they do not merge into an all-engulfing western modernism and globalisation process.

Without the support of education, trying to adapt these South Asian values into a western context was often inconsistent and confusing – especially when coupled with experience of rejection and racism.

Racism: confronting prejudice

There was plenty of evidence of people feeling up against institutional racism. P2 has this to say:

P2:   When you do go out there and when you do have to face these racial problems it's very difficult. You think well, after all colour matters as they say – it matters – it makes the difference ... It makes a huge – I think it makes all the difference. I mean I've had a lot of conversations on the phone and then I've gone to this certain place and then they've looked at me and thought that's not him ... and it hurts – it does hurt.

This rejection by the host culture can be internalised to become self-rejection. Kenneth and Mamie Clark's (1947) study of children's self perceptions revealed that Black children in the US sometimes identified themselves as White, implying that these children feel that their Black identity undermines their self esteem. Modood (1994) offers an explanation: Black (African Caribbean and Asian minorities) are responding to the negative response to their identities given to them by the host country.

In her study of refugee and Bengali communities, Patel quotes Thomas (1995):

> For Black young people, growing up in a White society or arriving in a totally different country can lead to this confusion. The experience of racism erodes self esteem and confidence, and a

young person can internalise the racism, and believe they are inferior to white society. (162:1997)

P1 described how racism affected the children in her community. She recognised that the differences were due to people's different perceptions and prejudice. She acknowledged the way in which Islam is perceived and how this can impact upon a child's identification with their religious identity:

P1:   Children don't want to say, 'I'm a Muslim' because there are stereotypical images and negative images of Muslims ... They might not want to be open ... because of racism ... They [children] need a lot of ... things [apart from just learning the Koran] ...

To prevent such self-disparagement caused by experiences of racism and feeling outcast, interviewees believed that knowledge about ethnic/religious identity was essential. Most thought that the challenge of living in western society made it vital for children to understand their cultures and religions well. P1 explains why it is important for the children to have good understanding of Islam as well as their cultural identity. They may have feelings of isolation created by a sense that people do not understand your world:

P1:   [They need] Somebody who understands their culture and religion ... then they don't feel isolated.

Racism alone does not account for the profound sense of isolation experienced by some families and often by women. The infrastructure of familial communication systems, rituals and institutions in Bangladesh or the Punjab that support a different arrangement of roles and responsibilities between genders do not exist in the UK.

Gender issues: studies on South Asian women

Wilson (1978) notes how families expect their women to uphold and preserve their culture and emphasises the social pressures on Asian women to conform. She describes the loneliness and depression which Asian women can experience when isolated from their extended family in India and feeling moral responsibility to observe strict cultural practices for their community in the UK. She notes how powerful communal networks are broken because of the geographical separation from the extended family abroad. Separated from the means by which these cultural practices are sustained can create a crisis for some women. One might expect that her analysis of the situation in the late 1970s would no longer apply thirty years on but there are many indications that problems of conformity and isolation continue.

In a composition of photographic images titled *Live for the Sharam and die for the Izzat,* Bhimji (1990) conveys the pain faced by Asian women torn between different cultures and ultimately no longer able to belong to either. Women facing such crisis could themselves be unable to address the same problem their children face. *Growing up young, Asian and female in Britain: a report on self-harm and suicide* (1998) funded by the Newham innercity multifund is one report which raises continued concern about the situation for a worrying number of young women. Batsleer, Chantler and Burman's (2003) *Responses of Health and Social Care Staff to South Asian Women who Attempt Suicide and/or Self-Harm* endorses this concern and indicates the disturbing response to the pressures these women face.

Although the communities offered a haven, a retreat from the confusions of the wider culture, they were also constraining and demanding. One parent said that it could feel like a parade ground and that she felt overpowered by her in-laws deciding what she could and could not wear. P1 explains that parents are 'are always being judged by the community; by our own families; by our elders', so restricting their moves to adapt certain customs to accommodate their children. Clothes were used as a means of control and this made people self-conscious about not fitting in:

B1:   If I was a Bangladeshi and not a Muslim I could mix in more ... like some people say it doesn't restrict you but in a way it does ... say it's a child's party and child's birthday party and you go in and say it's a summer's day and you see all these parents and they're there like in these tee-shirts.

Sikh girls had a different set of challenges to face and were afforded less clarity about issues of dress and codes of practice.

C10 (S) notes:

It's not that strict but it's quite strict because my nan doesn't like it when I don't cover my arms and things like that; she does want me to wear what I should wear ... she wants me to wear [traditional clothes] all the time but I don't want to, but only when I go to the Gurdwara.

It is not only females who can feel alienated; a lone Sikh boy in this study expressed anxiety about wearing his *bhagtah* (head-covering). But women, because they are representatives of their culture and beliefs through their dress and etiquette, face paradoxes presented by the West. The declaration of belonging through dress expresses levels of conformity that a western emphasis on autonomy can deride as inhibition of the freedom of expression or as subservience and dependency. The paradox lies in the degree of independence from the wider society demanded to express different values and beliefs through appearance. Western identity appears to allow for an expression of individuality and autonomy, but this turns out to be surprisingly limiting, apparently driven by capitalism. Dress in the West conveys money and fashion. The independence of expression is also associated with wholly different customs and ideologies: women are encouraged to expose the shape of their bodies and men are expected not to cover themselves in trinkets or wear dresses. So the South Asian women who wear South Asian clothes may be asserting their own independent values and beliefs which suggests they are coping, whereas some women who wear western clothes may be trying to avoid negative reactions from others.

Concerns arose about not fitting in with society's expectations in ways besides appearance. B1 described how a Muslim identity created barriers to integration and socialising in UK society, an experience connected with cross-cultural tension or conflict.

Cross-cultural conflict

Words like 'difficult', 'problem' and 'worry' recurred frequently. Different ways of life involve different codes of behaviour. Particularly disturbing were incidents when children reacted violently to being bullied. Parents who had expectations of 'good' behaviour and little understanding of what goes on in schools could not see that a bullied boy might behave in this way, B3 identified a misunderstanding of this kind:

B3:   It's the language. And my mother is suffering so much ... it's very difficult. My brother is very naughty sometimes and gets beaten up [outside school] and he doesn't go to school for a few days ... my mum [and dad] they can't understand why this situation is like this.

Several interviewees reported that language barriers created severe challenges for parents when their children were identified by the school as problematic, and intensified the sense of cross-cultural misunderstandings. Misunderstanding between parents, schools and society can create serious problems for young people. B1 acknowledges the dichotomies they face:

B1:   [The] culture is so different ... being a Muslim you can't go to nightclubs. You can't have boyfriends ...

P1 remarked on the expectations the communities had in relation to gender:

P1: Boys do go out with parents' knowledge because it isn't considered so dangerous for boys ... boys are encouraged more [to be educated] because they are going to be the breadwinners.

She noted that the community can add to a family's difficulties if their daughter wants to study away from home:

P1: Communities don't help because they'll come out with stories that my daughter went and she was away for three years and then she never came back.

When people are attempting to liberate themselves from what they feel are serious constraints within the communities, such lack of support contributes to the sense of isolation and 'difference' that participants expressed.

Feeling different and isolated

B1 was one of those who expressed feelings of difference, of being an outcast and feeling embarrassed because of her beliefs and customs. When these feelings surfaced in her life, her sense of difference made her feel isolated. B1 mentions a social gathering where 'I was the only Asian there'. She explained that it is not just appearance and rules that create this sense of difference but that 'It's this thing inside you; you feel different'. Dealing with the difference could also be embarrassing: 'I didn't open up and I pretended I had [things to do] to avoid socialising'.

The psychological repercussions of being different and having different priorities reinforced a sense that they were isolated by their difference. B2 explains this in the quote which opens this chapter.

Here she observes that it is not just the way people felt in themselves but also the uncertainty of westerners about how to respond to them. The language barrier can exacerbate these experiences of being different, as B1 explains:

B1: And there are other situations that result in feeling ... like an outsider. The reason they feel like an outsider is because of the language.

She went on to describe a situation in hospital where a Pakistani young woman went to have her baby. She did not realise that she could have Halal food and because she had little English she ate only salads.

The communities also faced the complex task of clarifying which cultural or religious practices should predominate. These differences relate to different aspects of daily life and were accentuated by their knowledge of what life was like in Bangladesh. B2 described the shock for Bangladeshis arriving in the UK when they found how privacy dominates over communality:

B2: When they come to this country there's not that hustle and bustle they're used to like over there – people go out and see anybody they want – people are more indoors over here. And they're more private.

Contrasting cultural expectations for children

Cross-cultural complications like those mentioned above are heightened in child rearing, since the generations have different experiences and expectations of it. Interviewees felt ostracised for being different and observed that their children had expectations of freedom of expression, learned from living in the UK society. Contrasting cultural expectations could clash, in a conflict between self-expression and cultural codes of behaviour. B3 was concerned about the confusion between parents and children over freedom of expression, choice and financial independence experienced by families living in the UK:

SCG: So he's [the participant's brother] become more assertive?

B3: Yes he is, he's very, very naughty.

SCG: So there's confusion?

B3: It's, they're confused because if they were in Bangladesh he wouldn't do all these things. He needs to be good person for himself and if he got beat up one day he wouldn't do all these things and say all these stupid things at the school or in the house. He wouldn't cause so much trouble for other people. He'd talk to them and they'd understand. So because he's in England he can say, he can call the police so that's the power children have and they're just spoilt with that ... because in Bangladesh they know home is home and there is nowhere else to go. There is no help outside of the home ... [but here] my brother can say fine I'm leaving home; they can say right I'm going now you don't listen to me, I'll go and live in a home.

This independence and the different behaviour affected the young people:

B3:   They're [the young people] not being the ones we want them to be. And the community might feel you should do the way we want. And the children who have been brought up here, they think: no we don't want to do that; we want to do what pleases me.

B2 elaborated on the confusions that can occur:

B2:   So children who've been brought up here don't agree with [the strict up- bringing on the Subcontinent] they don't work well with that. I often had to force ... [my daughter] to go to the Mosque and she's fought all the way ... so we had to talk to her teacher [at the Mosque] ... I think children brought up in this country expect a lot of freedom of choice ... parents are afraid ... they want more control over their children's lives but they have less and less control.

P2 was able to relate to the difficulties in his own experience as a youth.

P2:   Being born and brought up in this country is quite difficult at times to actually adopt our rules and regulations ... If you put those pressures on your children in their teens then you are go-ing to have problems.

Clearly, South Asian young people have a range of issues to face.

South Asian pupils' perspective on cross-cultural conflict

The pupils also expressed concern over prejudice in the wider society about their beliefs and practices. They had reservations about being UK citizens and of racism, which concerned them. They indicated a certain lack of identification with the locality they lived in, and expressed their fear of Islamaphobia:

SCG: Right so you like living here in [this area]?

C3(B), C5(B), C9(P): Yeh – it's alright.

C3(B):   It's a bit rough.

C5(B):   Yeh [the locality] is not a good area cos ...

C9(P):   Violence.

C5(B):   There's loads of like rules about how Muslims are like and that stuff. And they beat up – they sometimes kill the Muslims – the Christians ... Cos you know the police, do you know the police they don't do nuffin'. Police don't care; they don't know what is happening, they blame it on the Muslims.

The experience of being identified as different from the rest of society gave them problems as well as a sense of importance.

The pupils did not articulate the complex situation they experienced of living in close knit communities while being identified as different by British society. It was P3 who described the problems for young people living under the eye of their communities. She was a devout Muslim and although she mixed with western friends she did not relish the idea of their social life:

P3:   Being aware of the religion and how it helps us to lead a good life, it doesn't mean that if you socialise with other white people that you turn out to be one of them and go out clubbing. You must always be aware that you're Muslim as well and you stick to your values and culture.

Although clear about the importance of her Muslim values, P3 was also scathing about the insularity of her community and this made her position contradictory at times. Islamic and Sikh scriptures emphasise the importance of a spiritual and non-materialistic life and both Muslim and Sikh participants mentioned this priority. P2 declared that 'children don't want to see buildings or cars or wealth ... they just want a good life ... unfortunately people are very materialistic these days.' The growth in materialism was attributed to western influence. The participants also expressed a lack of affiliation at times with either British society or their communities. S2 criticised her community's superficiality and dishonesty and for emphasising appearance and denying the truth:

S2:   The community seems to be one big show of front that everybody's living in this way.

There seemed to be considerable gaps between the two main contrasting influences in the pupils' lives and no particular person with whom to address the disparities and problems that arose from cross-cultural conflicts.

Furthermore, generational differences affected the concept of openness, itself particularly complex in this cross-cultural situation. There were contradictory beliefs about whether to express feelings or observe traditional customs relating to decorum. B2 captured this quandary:

B2:   He [her brother] was visiting a family and they were dressed very formally, dressed up in a suit and things ... But when he turned up he was a bit casual I would say but they would say scruffy. He thought they should meet him in his ordinariness – it's the wrong idea isn't it? And my brother ... didn't want to lie about it so he said he didn't always go all the time to Mosque. And my aunties and uncles were saying 'Come on, go with them, just show them that you're interested [in an arranged marriage]'. And he wanted to be honest and straight.

Certain South Asian cultural expectations, religious beliefs and values are clearly incompatible with those in UK society. In particular, the sense of individualism and autonomy characteristic of western cultures may relate to degrees of isolation that originate from an ideological, cultural belief in the importance of independence rather than interdependence. Tolerance, belonging and emotional security were words the participants used to describe what a family should have. There was an implied criticism that UK culture encouraged indifference to family commitments and left people lonely and isolated. This research did not attempt to assess the reality of these aspirations and beliefs but it acknowledges that they are the ideals to which community members aspire. What was clear was that it took determination and courage for community members to gain acceptance of their practices in society as well as the school, as B2 articulates:

B2:   It's difficult. I mean if you want to do your *namas* [prayers] on time there is no place to do it ... you'd have to come home unless you talk personally to the headteacher of the school; or your employer ... some people don't feel brave enough to do it.

She went on to note the concern for parents:

B2:   We expect our children to listen to us and maybe stay in and not to go roaming around too much and we expect them to get on with their studies and respect their elders. I think they get a different picture outside of home ... my daughter she thinks life is only about going out with her friends and shopping and always watching TV all the time. And that's not what I want for her. I want her to remember to read the Koran and do her *namas*. But she thinks all those things are not important.

P2 was aware of the huge differences in lifestyles and belief and described how family and culture was crucial:

P2:   Colour, religion, just our whole way of life is completely different to the western way of life ... we have to follow a set of rules basically and that means towards our religion, our parents and even friends ... it's very difficult at times ... and possibly understanding of the way of life not only here but as well as Islamic and Pakistani side. It's very difficult for anyone unless you are a

Muslim/Pakistani to understand ... The number one priority in our culture is our family because we're so close knit and that's it really: to teach them [children] the family thing is very important as well as everything else. It's like most religions – you are taught that your priorities are: your religion comes first then it's your parents and then it's your neighbours, and then it's to respect all religions – they keep on repeating [in this order] which is a shame really.

P2 felt that a hierarchy of priorities could be too rigid but stressed that Islamic classes were understood by parents to be a priority:

P2:   [The] Islamic side of things is taken a lot more seriously and they tend to think that our Islamic side is a lot more important and it's a lot more disciplined, so it's more important.

Tensions were particularly acute over being religious in a secular society. The emphasis on attending the Mosque for instruction in Islam and Arabic put pressure on both the children and the community. Teaching in the Mosque differs from the teaching in school:

P1:   The reason is that they often have many children at one time and they've got one Imam teaching a good deal ... so obviously there's got to be some strictness there. Part of the practice you know comes back from Pakistan where they're teaching those methods there. ... Obviously [here] they've had a day at the school and then they go to the Mosque for one or two hours. Obviously it's a long day – they are shattered basically. They go into the Mosque and if they go to the Koran they know what page they are on and they'll go there, sit down, get to the page and start reading. And then when their time comes then they'll either go up to the Imam or he'll come to them. He'll listen to them and he'll move them forward and they'll go on to the next page and so on.

However, the Bangladeshi and Pakistani members (B2 and P2) both commented on changes needed in the Mosque to respond to children's experience of school. The Bangladeshi member felt that rules are too conspicuous in the Mosque and incompatible with children's expectations:

B2:   Teachers in the Mosque ... expect children to listen straight away; not answer back and if the children do answer back they'll be scolded ... we had to talk to them [the teachers in the Mosque and tell them that the children] need everything explained to them – not forced down their throat or anything like that.

P2 endorsed this concern about cultural clashes. However, change can be threatening for parents as they fear their lack of control, as B2 noted.

Different pedagogies and childrearing practices

P1 also spoke about the difference between Islamic studies and the pedagogy in the Mosque:

P1:   I don't know much about the Islamic studies because I've never been to one. But I know the teachers they have there would have more knowledge of the teaching methods used in schools. So I think they would be slightly more relaxed and they would have much smaller classes as well. And then I think that's because it's Islamic studies and there is more of a questioning – so more of a structured class. Whereas learning the Koran they go away and they're basically just sitting there reading through ... And it works – it works!

This comment seems contradictory. On the one hand P1 appeared to appreciate the more relaxed attitude in Islamic studies while on the other expressing enthusiasm about the results of a strict, un-compromising approach in the Mosque. There were not only peda-gogic differences but also underlying differences in the approaches to Islam. The Pakistani member (P2) was critical of fanaticism in some sects and suggested that there was a two-way interaction:

P2:   Yes it is a lot more fanatical here. I mean there are two Mosques here in ... the main two Mosques and they're always conflicting because in every religion everyone preaches differently. You know among Muslims there are so many different sects, that we all preach differently.

These issues of diversity exist at several levels: in relation to peda-gogy, location, the religion itself and then the contrast to a western approach present complex problems for parents. There are indications that there is much debate and difference of opinion among the Muslim population and the Bangladeshi Mosque differs from the Pakistani Mosques.

Sikh parents were also confronted with difficult decisions. S1 raised some of these issues:

S1:   Muslims – when their children are born from day one there are certain procedures that they go through ... Very clearly laid out and the children know what the procedures are and they know that this is what makes them Muslim. But in the Sikh community there isn't that. The children will just have to gradually grow into their religion ... we [Sikh parents] try to teach them to pray but then there's problems because again, with Muslims from a very early age they're taught how to read the Koran and Sikh children are not necessarily ... Unless there's a very devout Sikh. Like although we call ourselves Sikhs we can't actually – because in order to be devout we have to take our vows. And if we have taken our vows then within our vows we have a duty to teach our children about Sikhism.

S1 explains her anxiety because some people come to the Gurdwara with less commitment than others and:

S1:   It's so easy for you to lose your identity. I can see in the rooms downstairs- you can see people who've come to the Gurdwara because they've been asked or invited, you can see those completely aside from those who want to be there.

However she hoped that '[The] Giani [Sikh priest] ... from India ... can teach us about the Granths [holy book] and really lay down the foundation for our identity'.

S1 went on to suggest that young women were becoming more assertive about what they wanted to do: 'And she may say well I definitely want to go [to college or university]' and that mothers are learning to talk fathers around to the idea. 'Mothers will then try and talk the fathers round ... Again it's looking at the benefits for the daughters that – you know, if they are having an arranged marriage then if they've got an educated daughter then they are going to get an educated son-in-law'.

In this contradictory and compromised response, different cultural, social and religious beliefs can manifest in conflict and contribute to cross-cultural tensions in schools. Despite the challenges that the communities faced there were clearly developments as identified by S1 and others, that could enhance opportunities for both the communities' members and pupils in schools. The reflective, honest and challenging revelations that participants voiced have influenced the suggestions for sessions in schools.

Classroom sessions and activities to assist the contradictory and compromised response

The sessions that follow confront the disjunctures and tensions voiced by participants and explore possible solutions in the form of role models and ways of conceptualising conflict in society. This chapter is concerned with dissonance and conflict, awareness of difference and racism.

Sessions three and four are about:

- Looking at the challenge in difference: racism and negative stereotyping, power and inequality

- Conflict resolution: Considering Black role models and people who have fought against discrimination. Considering their character and qualities. Looking at school policies and practices relating to bullying and racism

The sessions look at various perspectives and adapting understanding: problem solving, empathising with other perspectives and experiences and also recognising inequalities. It is vital that the environment is safe and yet stimulating, so that children feel encouraged to discuss their concerns as well as diverse beliefs and practices. Should issues relating to racism be raised it may be necessary to identify a time after the session for children who have disturbing experiences to relate to discuss them in a more private situation. Sessions that open avenues to discuss racism and cross-cultural conflict can evoke emotional reactions so require care.

Playing a physically active game, where children move around and take on roles, can diffuse some of the tension. For example the children stand in a row and are asked to imagine that they represent different people in society: perhaps a young black man, a middle aged white woman, a young child with a disability. Then the teacher/ facilitator reads out various scenarios, such as applying for a job, walking down the street at night, going to the cinema, and asks them to step forward if they think they could do this easily. Once all the scenarios have been read out and the children are standing in different positions – some further forward and some at the back, the teacher/facilitator asks them to explain what they could or could not do easily and why. Similar explorations could be set up in drama, dance or music.

The key aims are to:

- look at disturbing feelings: being bullied etc.

- question and explore who we are and recognise that racism and inequality in society can cause tension

- deconstruct and demystify stereotypes, such as how Islam is viewed in the West

- compare and contrast UK culture with a South Asian culture

- examine grey areas and beliefs or practices that are ambiguous or unclear and the importance of questioning

- recognise and study the qualities of Black role models

- increase empathy and resolve socio-cognitive conflict: consider conflict resolution strategies

- develop equilibrium and problem solving ability

- increase ability to see our beliefs from a contrasting perspective

Introduce the sessions with reference to what was shared in the previous two: the importance of our sense of belonging and identity, how people's differences could be positive and interesting and how the next two sessions consider the sort of problems which can arise from people being different. To ensure an interactive session, it is useful to ask the children to consider what these might be. Then say that racism, exclusion, power, stereotyping, labelling and fear of differences exist in society.

Session 3 looks at feelings and thoughts and it is appropriate to introduce an exchange about feelings at the beginning of the third session. For example:

- How have you felt over the week?

- Has anyone felt ... this week?

- Is there anything else anyone wants to say or ask about feeling ... ?

Feelings need to be discussed before the children consider how people feel when they experience racism.

Play a DVD of biographies from a concentration camp. (One resource is the *Origins* video, see end of chapter two). Anne Frank's comment 'The time will come when we'll be people again and not just Jews,' can be considered and questioned. It is also valuable to gather ideas about why the Holocaust happened. Question beliefs such as 'all Jews are evil and corrupt'. Consider the local stereotypes of people, what sort of things people say – the names people are called. Trace how stereotypes of people can be the beginning of a process that undermines groups of people, in some cases culminating in genocide.

Then look at other groups who have been excluded and discriminated against. Ask the children to consider what they think people in the wider society say about their culture, religion, community or social background. Consider comments like 'Black people are stupid'. Discuss where these ideas come from and how they affect people.

Clarify the difference between bullying and racism. Consider who has power over us in the home, wider society and various situations. Note that misunderstandings can occur because people absorb and adopt stereotypes of others and do not question or consider another person's perspective imaginatively or empathetically so ignorance prevails. To illustrate the power of the media, find an article in a paper that endorses negative stereotypes of Black, Asian or other people. Refer back to Session 1 on celebrating diversity. Then question how people without power feel.

Children can be asked to problem solve and act out the following scenarios:

■ Marooned – lost your money in London; stuck in a forest storm in Pakistan; isolated in the playground with no one to play with; being chased ... Describe precisely how you feel and what help you need.

■ Significance – students bring in items, pictures, captions such as 'That boy is wearing a scarf on his head'. Discuss

---

The definitions are taken from Stella Dadzie's *Toolkit for Tackling Racism in Schools* (p94)

Racism – describes a complex set of attitudes and behaviour towards people from another racial or ethnic group, most commonly based on:

■ the belief that differences in physical/cultural characteristics (such as skin colour, language, dress, religious practices etc) correspond directly to differences in personality, intelligence or ability, leading to assumptions about racial superiority and inferiority

■ the social or economic power of members of one racial or ethnic group to promote, enforce or 'act out' such attitudes

Stereotyping – involves labelling or categorising particular groups of people, usually in a negative way, according to pre-conceived ideas or broad generalisations about them – and then assuming that all members of that group will think and behave identically.

what sort of life the boy leads, what he might think, what he would like

■ Discuss what qualities determine attractiveness in different cultures by looking at a variety of images of people wearing different clothing. Discuss why people wear different clothes and why expectations about what women and men should wear vary in different cultures

■ List five differences in the way of life that you have discovered about children from another culture

■ Relationships: To stimulate creative thinking, discuss how different people relate to each other and think about each other in various scenarios, eg. woman wearing shalwar kameez and a policeman

Session 4 focuses on conflict resolution strategies and role models of Black people who have fought racism. Highlight the achievements of Black and other ethnic minority people.

Watch a DVD featuring Martin Luther King, Mahatma Gandhi or Nelson Mandela. Consider how you would identify a role model. Pull out the qualities and attitudes of role models.

Include less well known role models, such as Fatima Jibrell who saved Somalia from the devastation of logging by charcoal exporters, or freedom fighter Hawa Tako (details about these role models can be downloaded via the internet).

Ask

Who has been a role model to you?

Why/What have they done?

Think of two questions you would want to ask a role model

'Hot-seating' the teacher. The teacher is asked to role-play a famous role model and the children ask questions such as: ' Why did you fight for independence?' What do you believe in?'

List and discuss the feelings and thoughts that came up when bullying and racism were discussed in the last session. Consider why there is bullying and racism and think of how you as a role model would deal with them, what you would do and say to people.

Review the school's race equality policy and evaluate its effectiveness.

Design a leaflet that offers advice as well as useful contacts for combating racism or/and bullying.

Other resources to draw upon

Robin Richardson (2005) *Here, There and Everywhere:*

History: learning that people from the colonies fought for Britain in both world wars eg. the Sikh gurkas

PSHE: The story of a 5 year old Iranian asylum seeker; imagine her likes, dislikes and worries

PE and dance: Football unites, racism divides – choreograph a dance performance on fusion and belonging

Runnymede Trust (2003) *Complementing Teachers:*

Citizenship: Feelings KS1; The Stephen Lawrence Inquiry KS2; Social and Moral Dilemmas: What to do? KS2; Becoming informed Citizens KS3; How to Keep the Peace in the World (the example is of the Israeli/Palestinian conflict but could be of conflict between western and non-western ideology eg Islam in Iraq contrasted with Christianity in America).

Migration Past and Present KS3; Why did Bashir Ahmed Abdi Die? KS3; A Fair Day's Pay KS4

History: Why do we remember Mary Seacole and Florence Nightingale or Mahatma Gandhi and William Wilberforce? KS1; Why did Africans, Asians and Caribbeans Join the British War Effort? KS3; What Caused the Passage of the 1964 US Civil Rights Act? How did Pakistan and Bangladesh come into existence? KS4

Personal, Social and Health Education: Wants, Needs and Rights KS3; Racism in Personal Writing KS4; The media Portrayal of Black People KS3; Racial Violence KS4

Religious Education: Making Moral Decisions/Religious and Material KS4; Peace and Justice/Religion and Conflict KS4

Conclusion

Although the responses in this chapter have emphasised the contradictory and often unresolved nature of the participants' experiences and thoughts, these responses must be seen in the context of circumstances, such as the intensification by the wider society of cross-cultural tension and disjuncture. S1 identifies a growing reflexivity among a few members of the communities, which could transform educational opportunities for South Asian pupils. However this depends upon whether the educational system provides pathways for connection. This is explored in the next chapter.

5

Education: the potential for intellectual and social engagement

S2:   Because living in England we have to ... get an education to be living in England and to get ahead more ... we're living two lives; we're living an Asian life and an English life.

S1:   Although they've [the local schools] got quite a large percentage of Asian and ethnic minorities ... There aren't any Black or ethnic minority teachers there ... no real role models ... You are failing your ethnic minorities because you haven't supplied that ... You think Sikhs are very thick because they can't get anywhere.

Teacher M   Taking it quite literally I'd like them to have a sound foundation in the 3Rs, hoping they'll do better academically ... I want them to have a clear sense of identity; I want them to be proud of their background and who they are. I want them to have self-confidence about themselves, about what they are.

The last two chapters considered how context, experience and understanding prompt certain responses among South Asian participants. This chapter concentrates on the challenges the educational system presents for the teachers and communities and the potential for change. The situation is complex. S2 is clear about the tensions she has to resolve and yet invests hope and ambition in the educational system. S1 identifies one serious lack in the schools. Teacher M acknowledges the importance of identity and cultural pride for pupils, as well as academic success. The chapter explores the insights of both the teachers and the communities, especially the teachers' contrasting perspectives, which help to clarify the situation in schools. Their views are set within the wider educational arena.

Education has the potential to stimulate cognitive, social, cultural and emotional awareness. It can engender creative thinking, facilitate understanding and help to process states of disequilibrium or intellectual dissonance. With a socially diverse population, it can provide the foundations for social flexibility and an openness to explore differences. Yet such linking and support through education was seldom realisable to the communities. At times the educational system actually exacerbated cross-cultural tensions by adding constraints that were not acknowledged. Luthra (1997) draws attention to the wider context that exists for the child and notes that cultural identities have diversified and increased in Black communities. He argues that 'the British educational system contributes little to shaping these [Black and Asian] identities. It has failed to provide intellectual tools for the young to analyse and locate diversity in a comprehensible and meaningful framework'(p33). Though potentially an opportunity for cross-cultural engagement, schools seldom delivered.

Institutional racism in schools

The school may not just patronise children and underestimate their academic aptitudes but also devalue their beliefs and practices. Children moving across cultures develop different identities which must somehow coalesce. If they clash, children are vulnerable to a sense of disequilibrium and alienation. In her novel Zadie Smith's (2000) character finds reading Shakespeare in school irrelevant to his identity. South Asian children and adults may feel that their South Asian identity and its meanings are denied or derided outside their communities and this makes it difficult for them to identify with British culture. 'In the hierarchical language of the west, what is alien represents otherness, the site of difference and the repository of our fears and anxieties,' says Rutherford (1990:10). An educational context that does not challenge its cultural and social hegemony does not deal with this chasm. The concerns raised by the communities, as detailed below, need to be understood within the context of their unequal position in the school/home relationship.

Historically, the British system takes a predominantly ethnocentric approach to education (Tomlinson, 1990; Rattansi, 1992; Troyna,

1986; Short and Carrington, 1996, Gillborn, 1998), and the secular has survived at the expense of the sacred (Qureshi and Khan, 1989). It focuses upon the technicalities of language and learning and leaves little room for reflection and debate. Thus cultural awareness becomes an awareness of 'British' concerns, emphasising neutrality or technicality rather than the reality of diversity, complexity and difference in the inner cities.

For schools to appreciate difference they need to take account of cultures in the locality in a sensitive way. The curriculum has to be broadened and the communities welcomed. Yet what happens is that schools largely dismiss and devalue the knowledge children bring from their communities and homes. Bourdieu's concepts of *cultural capital* and *symbolic violence* offer some explanation.

Bourdieu looks at the long-term effects of education and its meanings for society in general. He considers the socio-political complexities by which certain values and beliefs dominate over others. He describes how the educational system selects, disseminates and prioritises certain knowledge. He points to the qualitative difference between school and home cultural knowledge, stressing that cultural capital represents the dominant values, beliefs and customs to which people are encouraged to aspire.

> Students are not only users but also products of the educational system ... social origin exerts its influence throughout the whole duration of schooling ... the socially conditioned predisposition to adapt oneself to the models, rules, and values which govern the school system, in short, the whole set of factors that make pupils feel and seem to be 'at home' or 'out of place' in the school, result ... in an unequal rate of scholastic achievement between the social classes ... Thus the direct influence of the cultural habits and the dispositions inherited from the original milieu [home] is amplified by the multiplier effect of the scholastic streamings and channelings ... which trigger the second action of determinants, which are all the more potent because they are expressed in the specific logic of schooling, in the form of sanctions which consecrate social inequalities while apparently ignoring them. (1979:13-14)

Cultural capital is transformed into academic capital within the school context and reinforces the cultural values of the middle classes and the elite, as others may not have the resources to access it. Bourdieu describes the barriers they face: ' ... the economic and social yield of the educational qualification depends upon the social capital, again inherited, which can be used to back it up ' (Bourdieu,

1977: 48). This political insight into inequality clarifies why some people and some identities are included and others excluded.

The picture is further complicated by the value a person places on the prevailing cultural capital, as this largely depends on their identification with it. Children may know about western values and beliefs, but choose to draw upon alternative sources of knowledge. They soon learn that this knowledge is not accepted or respected in school but its value depends upon the recognition and respect placed on it by others as well as themselves.

Symbolic violence

To his analysis of the unequal position of *other* cultural capital within the school context, Bourdieu adds symbolic violence or symbolic power. In various ways such as through the educational system, the elite use language, arbitrary knowledge and symbols in a systematic way that makes them appear absolute and definitive. They legitimise their cultural capital but their symbolic power remains invisible. This systematic assertion of particular, select symbols and knowledge devalues and undermines other people's and groups' symbols and beliefs to the extent that others unconsciously perceive themselves and their values and beliefs to be inferior. Thompson (1992) observes how various institutions in society have mechanisms through which different products are allocated different values:

> The educational system provides a good example of this process: the development of this system involves a certain kind of objectification in which formally defined credentials or qualifications become a mechanism for creating and sustaining inequalities, in such a way that recourse to overt force is unnecessary. (p31).

The exclusion of local/particular identities can cause people to deny their own beliefs and customs to gain position, recognition and influence in society. And this power is dependent upon being accepted as a power:

> To understand the nature of symbolic power, it is therefore crucial to see that it presupposes a kind of *active complicity* on the part of those subjected to it ... symbolic power requires, as a condition of its success, that those subjected to it believe in the legitimacy of power and the legitimacy of those who wield it. (Bourdieu,1992, p23, original emphasis).

Domination may be difficult for the dominated to comprehend as this power is seen as arbitrary, not conscious:

> Symbolic power ... [is] almost magical power which enables one to obtain the equivalent of what is obtained through force (whether physical or economic), by virtue of the specific effect of mobilization – it is a power that can be exercised only if it is *recognised*, that is misrecognised as arbitrary ... Symbolic power, a subordinate power, is a transformed, ie misrecognizable, transfigured and legitimated form of other forms of power ... capable of producing real effects without any apparent expenditure of energy. (Bourdieu 1992, p170; emphasise in the original)

This cultural and social hegemony is complex and needs to be understood in relation to the wider curriculum, the pastoral, social and political struggles within the school setting and the educational system.

The symbolic power identified by Bourdieu is in some instances resisted. Blackledge (2000) provides one example in his examination of the construction of literacy in the school system and its power relations with a Bangladeshi community and shows how the community tries to deal with the power imbalance:

> Contributory factors to some minority groups' underachievement ... appear to result in the internalisation by minority groups of a sense of ambivalence with regard to their cultural identity and sense of powerlessness in relation to the dominant group ... it became clear that [Bangladeshis] ... were not actively valued by the school. That is, the mothers were regarded as 'illiterate' because their particular literacies did not fit with the school ... the parent is rendered *voiceless* by the school's failure to provide either bilingual teachers or trained interpreters ... the minority group ... wishing to self guard its language and culture, and fearing assimilation, turns in on itself and rejects the form of education imposed by the majority group. (p55-67, my emphasis)

Institutional racism is apparent in central and local educational policies. Gillborn (2003) argues that government educational grants to schools of £155 million in 2003 to improve ethnic minority educational performance is high risk because schools are still institutionally racist, holding low expectations of their black pupils (Schopen, 2003). Acktar (2006) finds central government educational initiatives for urban Black communities to be: short-term, fragmented, endorsing a sense of impermanence, and failing to tackle racism.

Low expectations characterise delivery and not just policy, and there is institutional racism in teacher education.

Teacher recruitment and training

Teacher recruitment and training does little to overcome the home/ school divide. Teacher training in English for the National Curriculum, for instance, ignores the social process of literacy, so promoting a curriculum that reinforces ethnocentric views (Blackledge, 1998). And teacher training programmes have been criticised for their insensitivity to racism and cross-cultural concerns (eg Millett 1998). Jones *et al* (1997) found that ethnic minorities avoided teaching as a profession, not only because of its low status, but because chances for promotion were poor for Black teachers. In 2000 Spencer reported a serious shortage of ethnic minority teachers and noted that those in the system are still only expected to work in inner city areas. In 2004 the DfES achieved their target of 8% ethnic minority recruitment, the Initial Teacher Training Bursary Initiative 2004 helped to raise the recruitment of ethnic minority students to teaching ranging from 16% – 22%, but it is retention that will determine the outcomes for schools.

Teacher expectations

Teachers' expectations have been shown to contribute to the home/ school divide. Grant and Brooks (1998) demonstrate that government legislation is not dealing with inherent prejudice towards black children in the British educational system and to conflictual relationships between teachers and black students. Jones *et al* (1996) found that ethnic minority PGCE students on placement encounter racist attitudes: in one school, for instance, some teachers believed that all ethnic minority pupils have English as an additional language.

A more representative teaching force is only part of the solution to racism in schools. Black teachers may have greater insight into the situation for ethnic minority pupils and parents but combining insight with the responsibility to be a role model puts them under pressure (Jones *et al*, 1996).

There is a danger in assuming that South Asian teachers automatically understand and identify with all the communities. Teachers in general, South Asian or not, may have assimilated stereotypical views of minority groups. While they may well represent role models for the communities, they come from a range of social backgrounds so will have varied values and perspectives. Even the two teachers in this study differed in their knowledge and attitudes towards the South Asian parents and communities, and this affected the way the parents related to them.

Introducing the teacher participants

Although the South Asian participants in this study were embedded in their communities, the teachers (M and X) of South Asian origin who worked in the local schools lived outside the area of the school and did not mix with the community. These teachers of South Asian descent were accountable to the school and trained in the British educational system. Their responsibilities for meeting government requirements affected their role as representatives of South Asian communities.

My interviews with them explored the aims for pupils, cultural differences, attitudes to achieving well, contact with parents, differences with parents, the experiences of South Asian pupils, other issues including the National Curriculum and Ofsted.

Teacher M

Teacher M teaches in the main school but does not live in the neighbourhood among the local community. Brought up in South Asia, she is familiar with the values, beliefs and life-styles of the communities although some of her opinions differ from theirs. She sees herself as more western and she is neither Muslim nor Sikh but Hindu. She regards herself as a non-believer and, she is glad that her religion has a place for people like herself. Interestingly, when she talked about South Asian culture she used the word *our*, revealing her affiliation with South Asian cultures. She respected religion and recognised its importance but was concerned about what she saw as the fundamentalism in the communities, as dangerously fanatical and characterised by indoctrination. She summed up her general stance:

Teacher M: I've probably grown up within the western educational system and I have western views ... There are lots of questions that I have no answers to. Questions like death and life and God.

Teacher X

Teacher X worked in the pilot school. She, too, lived outside the area. She grew up on an island in the Pacific in a small family unit that lived separately from others on the island and her parents were not particularly religious. She did not experience the extended family set-up, but her parents did have some values in common with South Asian communities – with which she disagreed. She was sensitive to issues of equal opportunity, and critical of the ways the National Curriculum inhibited her from helping her pupils acquire the life skills she felt they needed. She understood that the children came from an inner city area and faced various disadvantages. But she expressed frustration with the Asian communities because she had never been part of a close knit community and was unimpressed by its insularity.

Although teacher X expressed tensions similar to those of teacher M she could not affiliate with the South Asian communities and their religious values and beliefs as teacher M did:

Teacher X: I feel very different to the Asian community. I don't feel part of the Asian community – I don't feel I'm welcomed as part of the Asian community ... Because of being brought up in a really small family unit with no extended family; that's the frame of reference that I had and not overly religious.

The teachers' aims for pupils

Teacher M: Taking it quite literally, I'd like them to have a sound foundation in the 3Rs hoping they'll do better academically and settle into professions they want to do. I want them to do well academically but more importantly I want them to have the right values. I want them to have a really good sense of discrimination and to be able to understand the difference between right and wrong ... to be able to make choices. And I want them to be proud of who they are because a lot of our children come from the ethnic minority groups.

Also, her desire to help the pupils to develop pride in their identity and background as well as for them to do well academically gave teacher M strong links with the ideals of the South Asian parents, as we shall see. But moral education could be an area of contention with parents:

Teacher M: I want my children at school to be open minded, more tolerant ... I think when I'm talking about the Muslim religion ... to me it's almost a sort of brain washing style. Children blindly follow things, without questioning, without looking at things at a deeper level.

She was suspicious of fanatical elements in Islam and thought some of the parents espoused such views. Teacher X had somewhat different ideals:

Teacher X: I want to give them [my pupils] a sense of independence and [for them to] be able to get on by themselves and use the knowledge and skills that they've got and apply them to various situations that they are going to come across in their lives; to give them loads of advice and practical information. Not just focusing on the core subjects, although I know that teaching now is all numeracy and all literacy and that's fine, but it doesn't help the children with life skills; to get on with other people and communicate effectively with each other. And I think my role as a teacher is to help them communicate their ideas and feelings and aspirations, to get what they want in a co-operative way. Especially in a school like ... where competitiveness is avoided because of the nature of the children themselves.

Teacher X believed that the children faced basic disadvantages. She focused on independence and the ability to communicate in relation to the racial and economic disadvantages her pupils faced. By contrast, teacher M stressed moral values, ethnic pride and confidence in terms of personal, community and academic values as aims for her pupils, which was closer to the South Asian parents' interests.

Cultural differences

Teacher M recognised the cultural needs of her pupils and tried to adapt the curriculum accordingly:

Teacher M: English, English is predominantly British but we also do a lot of non-standard English. We sometimes deal with word order and bring in other languages, especially the languages the children bring with them – just to heighten their interest in languages and grammars. We naturally do our best rather than a conscious effort to make it a multicultural education. The students themselves come from such different places that we do try to incorporate cultures from different parts of the world.

She felt that their cultural background was an asset:

Teacher M   I'd like them to know about our culture because in that way India has a lot to offer. In that way I'd like them to know more about our culture, more about our history and more about our religion. I come from the Hindu religion and although I'm not being extremist (*with a laugh in her voice*) I must admit it's a very tolerant religion; open-minded religion. It has a place for non-believers like me (*she laughs and so do I*).

Teacher X, in contrast, said nothing about the cultural needs of her South Asian pupils.

Attitudes to academic achievement

There appeared to be a divide with the parents over the different attitudes to education and their feelings about tests. Teacher M felt that the parents lacked understanding and just cared about getting things done:

Teacher M: I don't think South Asian parents, especially those living in [...] are aware of the education system here, nor the one that they've come from and there too they have a very shallow knowledge of the systems there. To them, doing well means doing well academically with their reading, writing and maths. So if you say your child shows a lot of flair in dance and music they're not as pleased as if you say she's exceptionally good at maths – then they feel really good about it. I think they're quite happy to see their children get homework ... they don't consider reading a book as homework or listening to the news and jotting down notes as homework. They want a formal set piece of paper and ... they keep asking: can you send more homework? So they're ready to support with that – just ensuring ... that the child does that.

Teacher M felt the parents' concern with tests was another issue on which they did not agree:

Teacher M: Most of the parents aren't aware of things and as they come from a culture where tests are OK so they think that their children come to school to learn Maths, English and Science and to improve their chance at tests.

But she empathised with the parents' concerns and understood that their differences were related to different ways of thinking and a lack of questioning:

Teacher M: I think a lot of our South Asian cultures don't develop the habit of questioning among individuals. It's always accepting what you receive, not questioning things. I think that is the big difference I find between eastern and western education. In the West you're taught to question all the time.

Teacher X also observed that South Asian parents were primarily interested in tests and exam results and she too disagreed with this focus:

Teacher X: I think they are relatively happy with the testing ... they are the parents who are happy to get in extra tuition and make sure their children go to homework club ... they put a certain value on passing exams ... I don't think that there is much concern for the Arts.

It was clear that both teachers had quite different understandings to the parents about the potential of education to develop skills and abilities.

General differences between parents and the teachers

Despite her reservations about the parents' interests, teacher M could anticipate what the parents would want to know if they came to PTA meetings:

Teacher M: [They want] a broad general statement about how they're doing work-wise and behaviour-wise.

However, her inside knowledge made her aware of the reasons behind some of their responses. She noted the parents' fears least western culture take over their children's value systems:

Teacher M: I think parents are quite scared that their children are going to go to the other extreme and become completely anglicised in their way of life and therefore they're hanging on to the old way of life and culture from back home. So therefore are pulling in that direction just to stop the children from becoming too westernised.

This helped her understand why the communities tended to stay together:

Teacher M: I think this sense of belonging becomes all the more intense because you know that otherwise you get isolated in a foreign land – so you stick together.

However, she was concerned that this intense focus on belonging together influenced the parents to try and keep too tight a rein on their children, which could have a detrimental effect. She also felt that pressures on the children were intensified because they were expected to attend lessons at the Mosque after school:

Teacher M: I'd say most parents do train their children into what is right and wrong because it's just part of our lives and it just happens at home. But there is such a strong influence of society of the outside world around them – so that the moment the children get away from their parental constraints, they try to follow the examples of their white and other friends and the behaviour outside school can be appalling. A lot of the children spend at least a couple of hours at the Mosque after they leave school. They do their prayers everyday and their whole life revolves around their religion; it does play a big part in their lives.

In her view, the pupils would be different to other pupils because of the pressures upon them. Teacher X did not identify with the interests and concerns of the South Asian parents in the same way and separated herself from them. She spoke about the degree of separation and lack of understanding between the communities and school.

Teacher X: If the Asian community was a bit more open it might be easier for people to get a better understanding ... it's very insular [the community], it's very small and it's very unwelcoming ... It really does seem to be very, very religious based and people will give children the opportunity to spend a lot of time out of school to do Arabic exams – to do – that and they don't seem to attach much value to the state education system ... it is only the Asian parents that are withdrawing their children for that period of time ... They want their children to get 'A' grades and to go to universities; they want their children to be professionals and at the same time they're not prepared to put the input in themselves ...

The teachers' views on the differences encountered by South Asian pupils

Teacher M was conscious that the South Asian parents' anxieties influenced their children's behaviour in school. When questioned about the effectiveness of the parents' close rein on their children, she replied:

Teacher M: No, completely opposite effect on things. I think the minute the children are away from home they are rebelling ... I see lots of Gujarati girls going with boys from a completely different race and culture ... I've known quite a few girls who have veils on and are wonderfully devout Muslims and once they're out they behave completely differently ... I am aware that many of our Muslim children are very, very Muslim almost to the point of extremism. If somebody were to say something that was in any way anti-Muslim they would be prepared to kill that person ... I'm not suggesting to them that they should forget about their religion. I think religion is a wonderful thing if you can believe in it. But to believe in it so much that that you believe everything else is trash is not right.

Despite teacher M's fears and concerns she understood the pressures of living in a cross-cultural situation and what this might mean for her pupils:

Teacher M: Yes it's a really tricky balance between things. On the one hand you're saying you should have your self identity and your individuality and on the other you're saying you need to be self- effacing and blend into the family structure, which may be a really extended family. I think there is a very big difference between eastern and western values and I don't know what happy balance you can strike.

Teacher X, on the other hand, was most concerned about the social and economic factors that disadvantaged South Asian children and tended to ghettoise them in certain areas:

Teacher X: The Asian children are seen as separate and it's the age-old thing that you run the shops and are segregated ... when you look at the housing and see how housing is arranged it is very distinct ... Very near the school a lot of White children live and a bit further away is where the majority of Asian people live.

Yet despite her criticisms of the parents, she was sympathetic to what she felt their children had to endure. She respected their endeavours but saw their problems as ultimately no different from other children's:

Teacher X: Yes – they work hard when they're in school, they're dedicated and focused and then also again when they go home. And they see it – I don't know but I presume that they see it as two very separate things that don't mingle

> with each other and school is one thing and home is another thing. And it's like that for a lot of children and it doesn't matter about their cultural background.

Despite X's awareness of the unequal educational opportunities provided for ethnic minority children, she didn't seem to realise – as teacher M did – how important and different a South Asian identity could be. She expressed surprise at the pupils' interest in their specific cultural identity when she was teaching about India in class:

Teacher X: It's funny you know because we did a topic on India, and all the South Asian children wanted to talk about was not India. India had absolutely no relevance at all. What they wanted to talk about was the Punjab and Pakistan. There were political issues to do with when Pakistan was first born. The one thing that a couple of Asian Sikh children in my class were really interested in was the Temple at Amritsar ... the political issues to do with the British leaving ... I think the main focus is religion.

However, when pressed about why she felt the pupils may have reacted in this way she did express an understanding:

Teacher X: To not forget where they come from and to not forget about their religious roots ... because I think people feel that they need the support of their own communities.

It seems that when they talked about the broader differences between South Asian pupils and other pupils, teacher X focused on the socio-economic and teacher M on cross-cultural factors.

Contact with parents

Teacher M expressed her disappointment and sense of powerlessness at her failed attempts to get to know the South Asian parents. She knew that the parents' lack of questioning and their expectations of their parental roles affected their involvement with the school:

Teacher M: Even if they don't understand. They don't question the system; they think the school is supposed to know what they're [the children] doing so they'll agree with everything they're saying. ... I don't expect any parents to turn up [to parents' evenings] ... I think much of it may be because they've got other younger siblings at home to look after, or a father-in-law or mother-in-law, so it's all the household chores, and there is no time to go and sit with your child. What you want is your child to be at school, so that you can get on with the other things you have got to do.

However as a parent herself, teacher M understood the difficulty in getting to PTAs: 'I don't have a minute – I don't even make it to parents' evening'. Teacher M clearly felt frustrated by the demands of the government:

Teacher M: I'll tell you about my experience (*laughs*). Recently be-
              cause of the government dictates, the school and parents
              had to sign a contract and that was to be done on parents'
              evening. And most of the parents that turned up were
              white parents and a couple of Bangladeshi parents and
              one Pakistani. It's supposed to be an agreement between
              the school and the parents/community and the parents
              have to say how they can contribute to their children's
              education and hardly any of the South Asian parents ever
              returned their forms. They never turn up for parents' even-
              ings ... you're never quite sure if it is getting through; or
              because they think this is another piece of paper to get out
              of the way.

She believed that meeting and liaising with parents was important but had difficulty communicating with them:

Teacher M: Ideally I think I'd like the parents to know what we are
              teaching in school; generally an idea, an awareness of the
              school day and the school routine. I don't think most
              parents know, neither are they interested. We send a lot of
              letters home on a termly basis. They don't get home be-
              cause the children don't think their parents will read it, or
              it's not important enough ... On parents' evening they're
              [the children] the ones that are translators ... [also] I can't
              always explain to the parents what level – three or four – I
              would want the child to reach. I can't open the National
              Curriculum document and say – level three means being
              able to ... plus it's meaningless.

Like teacher M, teacher X felt frustration with the South Asian parents' lack of attendance at PTA meetings and the difficulties of having to translate information through pupils (although there was translation support at the school).

Teacher X: I think it's to do with communication. You know we have
              one person in our school, who isn't a member of our staff,
              who comes from EMAS [the ethnic minority achievement

service] who does translation for us. One person for a school of 400 pupils which is not a good situation because parents are not going to come and sit in front of you and talk about their children because they don't have a grasp of the language. And it's not an ideal situation to have the child translate for you ... You don't really want to be giving the message to an older sibling ... They're [PTA meetings] important because they tell the parents how the children are getting on, what is to be done, what areas the children are lacking in, what areas they're doing really well in ... And it's important to get their opinions about what they think is going well and what is not going well. When we have parents' evenings the parents that are least likely to turn up are the Asian parents.

But she understood why Black parents, including South Asian parents, might be prevented from getting involved with the school in any substantial way:

Teacher X: I think it's to do with the fact that schools and educational institutions are not welcoming places for people who don't feel secure about their own ability to communicate ... I do feel as a school we could do a lot better to invite people on the management committee and onto the PTA but all of these things are run by a clique of may be half a dozen white parents – it's very exclusive and they don't allow other people to come in ... We've always got places available on our management committee ... we've only had two Asian people ... But it's like anything else ... it's very, very cliquey. So you know if you already feel threatened; you are not going to put yourself into a position where you feel even more vulnerable; where you are going to be the only voice that is saying – you don't want to put yourself in that position ... I mean I think it's a really, really sad situation that we don't try more ways of encouraging Asian parents to come in and be part of the school you know. And a lot of it is down to the fact that we don't have time.

Teacher X recognised that the school's lack of connection with South Asian and particularly the Islamic communities could be a great disadvantage at crucial times when there were opportunities to look at different religions and they were not represented. But her criticism of the school was somewhat contradicted by her ambivalent attitude to South Asian parents. Her sympathies fitted the school's point of view rather than the communities':

Teacher X: No we don't have any Asian parents who volunteer to do anything within the school – um. No, not really. They don't come in and offer their skills and that's not for want of being asked.

Although some of the South Asian parents had expressed appreciation of her as an Asian member of staff, she believed that they saw her as no more than part of the school institution:

Teacher X: Some of my parents will say that they're so pleased ... that ... they do have an Asian member of staff ... it's just another Black face ... . that is as far as it goes because there isn't that exchange or there isn't that communication. I think they see me as part of the establishment.

Clearly both teachers had institutional constraints that intensified their lack of communication and connection with South Asian parents. It was not only the teachers who had different views of parents; so did the schools themselves. The teachers were asked to identify which of Nicholls' (1999) three options described how their school encourages parents' involvement. In a school focused option, parents are involved with fund raising and governing; in a curriculum focused option they are expected to help with their children's homework and help in the classroom. But in a parent-focused attitude, the school regards parents as important educators in their own right. Teacher M thought her school took the final option, whereas teacher X thought her school followed a curriculum option. The teachers communicated with the parents according to the option adopted by the school, and this in turn influenced expectations about the parents.

Lack of relevant staff training

Teacher M was particularly concerned about the lack of training for staff about cultural issues and the conflicts that could arise, and was perturbed that other issues were considered more important:

Teacher M: I had a recent retraining on road safety and people from the road safety department came and they said that the school needs to take on the responsibility because parents weren't pulling their weight and I'm sure this applies to this area ... [but] ... I don't know if this is relevant but one of the Jamaican girls in my class was making fun of a child's name and she didn't realise that the child's name was also the name of the prophet. So just as you would say Nicky Picky, she was saying Abdullah Bukdulla – something like that – and she got beaten up at dinnertime by a lot of Muslim boys. And they said that she'd better prepare a grave, and be prepared to get buried after school that day and she was so petrified that she stayed in class until her mother came to collect her.

And then I spoke to the class and I said – she knows nothing about Muslim religion and I'm sure what she said had nothing to do with an attack on the religion. I said of course it's not right to make fun of somebody's name but have you all never called anybody a name? And they said – yeh, yeh we have. I said I'm sure it's something that can be forgiven isn't it? And she said sorry and I thought this was the end of the matter and come the next play-time she was brutally beaten up by the same group of Muslim boys again and that made me so cross because they seemed to agree with everything I said ... It is such a difficult issue that as a teacher I wouldn't want to deal with it unless I had the training. I don't have the training to do it. I think I understand the conflict that goes on within them better than someone that hasn't experienced the conflict within themselves ... Is it the curriculum that disallows the schools from addressing it? I don't know what it is? I think the school thinks our responsibility is mainly academic and that is all we can cope with ... In [this school] we spend about fifty percent of our time dealing with pastoral issues, I mean it's unending.

Teacher X felt inhibited by the lack of time and funding allocated to addressing the requirements of bilingual pupils. But she welcomed how EMAC (ethnic minority achievement consultants) had creatively developed positive relations between parents and schools:

Teacher X: EMAC teachers which are absolutely brilliant. But there is actually no time to get these things in. Parents come in and they make books with their children or they make games with their children. It's really to develop the parents' language which is really, really wonderful, it's really good but the school is saying that we may not have the resources to be able to offer this next year.

She was, however, concerned that recent funding supported the interests of African Caribbean pupils to the detriment of issues concerning South Asian pupils:

Teacher X: There doesn't seem to be any concern about putting into place any structures or systems to help children with problems that children might [have] who have ESL I think this is a lot due to the fact that schools are now very, very target driven ... to get our SATs results up we target those children in years 5 and 6. But the emphasis this year seems to be on um – I quote, 'disaffected Black children.'

In general though, she felt that equal opportunity, rather than the particular interests of specific ethnic minority groups, was the most important thing. And she saw South Asian children in terms of a broader socio-economic problem:

Teacher X: I mean at ... we do get a lot of children who have extreme behaviour. So we tend not to do competitive things with them although they learn such a lot playing competitive games. We do sharing activities – so just to give them life skills ... I mean a lot of children [here] ... come from very difficult backgrounds ... It's very difficult because so much time is spent on numeracy and literacy and it doesn't focus on children with ESL. It's very difficult for those children because they get more and more panicked because as a teacher you just do not have the time [to help them].

These concerns related to a variety of organisational and curriculum issues.

Targets, tests and Ofsted

Teacher M was concerned that the National Curriculum left so little opportunity to address issues of equal opportunity and cross-cultural tension:

Teacher M: They do have tokenistic bits on equal opps but the book is so thick that all you're interested in is on finding out what you have to teach. You're not worried about the SEN [special educational needs] about it.

The various problems she had experienced with the communities were exacerbated by restrictions of the National Curriculum. She found the tests and their preparation demanding and undermining to her relationship with her pupils:

Teacher M: Oh, its so ugly – I absolutely hate it. But in early January I've been to a couple of training courses where teachers from around [locality] come in to discuss how we can boost the children's results and so on. And the fever really begins to build up, and even though you try not to get the children stressed about it you cannot help mentioning at least twenty times a day – in the SATS you would do this: in the English SATS you would do this. I think since February we have dropped the National Curriculum and focusing only on Maths, English and Science because every school wants to achieve certain targets results-wise. And there's a big build up and the children hate it, I hate it and the parents who are aware of this come in and let me know how miserable it is making their children.

Despite these constraints teacher M used every opportunity to include culturally relevant material for her pupils:

Teacher M: I try to adjust my ways to suit the children's needs and follow the National Curriculum at the same time. In one curriculum area like history a lot of the topics are to do with European or British history but there is probably one fifth of it that deals with histories of other cultures. And we have a choice of West African States or Indus valley and we generally take the Indus valley because so many of our children come from Pakistan and Bangladesh. So we do quite a detailed study of this in year six. So there is some scope for this in certain subject areas. Being a school where there are so many ethnic groups you cannot help bringing in some of their cultures and languages into what you do. A lot of our RE celebrations, and even in assemblies teachers do themselves focus on different cultures, religions and languages.

In general Teacher M had insight into the limitations of the parents, their relative ignorance of the school curriculum, their emphasis on homework and tests. She appeared frustrated by both the South Asian parents and the National Curriculum requirements. Though aware of problems she seemed unable to resolve them. A sense of compromise and constraint pervaded the interviews despite her understanding and the important initiatives she took.

Teacher X also felt under pressure from Ofsted and the National Curriculum and was critical of the curriculum's irrelevance to the pupils' lives. This added to her difficulties with the South Asian communities:

Teacher X: Our work is already created for us. It's not coming from the children ... you can't always address the things that the children are having difficulty with within the strategy that the Government has developed. For you to address those needs what they say is that it's like a rolling programme so that every year or every term you come back to visit these things and there is the opportunity for you to do that. But for me as a teacher it makes more sense for me to address the issues as soon as you become aware of them ... But because of the constraints of the strategies you can't ... it's a national document and you as a school are lumped in with everyone else in the country to meet particular targets [but] we live in a world that is made up of all these different cultures; and we have to respect everybody in their different ways for their different beliefs. There is no time in the curriculum ... It's a very, very test-driven situation ... It does affect the atmosphere because it affects how you teach, it's that you are teaching to a test. That is what you teach to because with performance-related pay and all of these things that are coming in now – your salary is linked to how your children do ... Teachers are under so much pressure during that Ofsted week ... we specifically asked for a multicultural team when we had our Ofsted and we didn't get that ... there were no Black people on the team; there didn't seem to be awareness of Black issues. ... I think the thing that interests them most – Ofsted the most – is how a school is doing in its tests.

Teacher X recognised the lack of equal opportunity in Ofsted's appraisal. There were clearly issues and contributions that were completely overlooked or misinterpreted by the statutory assessment system upon which everything was judged. So her situation too was compromised and constrained. She too expressed concern about the Eurocentric content of the curriculum but found ways to adapt it:

Teacher X: The text that they give you is already written down for you ... and very few parts of the text come from other cultures. They're very, very Eurocentric, even in fact very, very British ... mean I think it has huge implications for those children who are not born in this country or whose parents were not born in the country. ... Primary school education in England does not help children who are not white to identify with the curriculum, like history; for instance if you take what we are supposed to do with the Victorians it has absolutely no relevance or bearing for children who are not white. It's all very white ... . When I teach I always talk

> about colonialism and the empire and things like that. It's all about the Industrial Revolution but from a British point of view and those sorts of things, so we are not making use of the resources we have in our communities ... if issues come up in the classroom ... then I will deal with those; I will make time to do that. And what suffers is my artwork ... my philosophy about education and about life is not about that ... And I think that's come from being born here and seeing how hard it is for Black people.

Both teachers were so constrained that, despite their insights, they could not resolve the concerns they raised, although they did use their initiative and imagination to reach beyond the limitations of the National Curriculum.

Although all the participants in this study are of South Asian origin this does not necessarily give them a connection; in fact the *impasse* between the school and communities alienated the teachers. The South Asian teachers felt they were in conflict with the communities' other priorities. So although these two Asian origin teachers potentially share with the parents concerns about equal opportunity, the demands of their jobs and the dictates of the National Curriculum left little room for sharing any understanding with the South Asian parents in the study. It is telling to compare this with studies which describe the benefits of Muslim schools (Parker Jenkins, 1995) or Sikh schools (Klein, 2000: 10) that combine cultural/religious knowledge with high academic attainment in the National Curriculum.

The lack of sharing registered by the teachers and parents in this study was endorsed by the lack of confidence, knowledge and opportunity the communities experienced in their relationship with the school (also see Vincent, 2001). The participants voiced concerns about the PTAs, curriculum content, cultural concerns, lack of role models, and the pupils and their priorities.

Problems with PTAs

The crucial point of contact between the school and parents was the PTAs but parents invariably found them alienating. B2 argued that it was not the parents who were at fault but the school system. She described the anxieties and embarrassment faced by parents at PTA meetings:

B2: My neighbours across the road they don't usually go because of the language problem. They have been and ... it's been very difficult for them and they've just wanted to go

> home ... they wanted to say things to the teachers but they just couldn't ... [they felt] very odd because people were looking at the way they were dressed ... when they talked, they talked with an accent and everyone was looking at them ... They were so embarrassed at that meeting.

This illustrates the general sense of isolation felt by the participants in relation to society and how this is intensified and reinforced by their experiences in schools. Communication problems arise especially when English is not their first language and are intensified by the parents' economic and cultural pressures. P2 explains how these responsibilities surface:

P2: The problem is that the only reason that they [parents] don't get involved the way they should do is because the man is always working. He puts everything on the wife and the wife might not even understand English but she has to attend the parents' evenings or let's say festivals, any concert or anything social in the school. But the father's always working so he's not really informed; all he does look at is the school report and whether it's good or bad and either they'll [the children] get punished or whatever. It's very sad.

As we saw in the contradictory and compromised response, parents like B2 and P2 were concerned about parents not attending PTAs but could not deal with the predicament from their position. However, P2 was aware that limited knowledge of the school's expectations disadvantaged both the parents and their children.

Parents' lack of knowledge of the educational system

Parents may have little understanding of the kind of knowledge and questioning pedagogy their children experience in the educational system. So intergenerational tensions are exacerbated. Luthra (1997) argues that although South Asian parents may be able to pass on folk culture to their children, they might have had insufficient education to transmit intellectual values within a rational framework. They may prefer a limited, authoritarian teaching style:

P1: [In Pakistan] not many schools have parental involvement and those are probably schools that follow ... [the] English system and those are usually private schools. So parents don't usually have involvement. They [do however] have involvement with their children's work at home; they get a lot of homework out there, and parents will make sure they'll get through those and they'll help if they can. I think they have the same thought here.

The Curriculum

Parents felt their values and beliefs were denied or undermined in the school.

B1 was concerned about the dominance of British culture and history in the curriculum:

B1: When our children go to school they just learn about the western things like whether it's history or whether it's English. It's all to do with like western culture; nothing to do with like Bangladeshi culture. I mean if an English child knew in depth the values and how important a culture is; if they [the teachers] told them [the children] ... that a Muslim girl has to cover her head; she has to wear appropriate dressing that has to go to her ankles and has to cover her arms and they're not allowed to drink at all – it's *haram* for them to drink; that they can't enter pubs ... and you have this thing about explaining, explaining, explaining.

Her views are confirmed by the research. For example Parker-Jenkins (1995) writes: 'British state schools and educational policy is seen as inconsistent with their [Muslims'] way of life ... Muslim parents aspire to keep their children faithful in the face of perceived Western imperialism and permissiveness' (p13). The curriculum reinforces a disparity between what South Asian children learn at school and what they have learned at home.

B1 saw how the focus on a 'British' curriculum reinforced the school's ignorance of her culture. Similarly S2, though enthusiastic about the school her children attended, was disappointed to find nothing about Sikhism in the curriculum and saw this as unhelpful. She feared for her children's knowledge of their roots and identity:

S2: I'm quite happy with the education, the only thing that worries me is ... Sikh education and it would be great if they could have that at the school.

The strain of trying to maintain a culture and religion that was seen as alien troubled all the South Asian parents.

Cultural concerns

S1 recognises that her children's links with Sikh culture are more tenuous than her own or her parents'. S2 also expressed concern that her children had less knowledge and understanding of Sikhism than she would like:

S2: Ways are kind of disappearing ... like at the time when we got married, everything was like arranged marriages and nowadays you hear things about people marrying outside religion and they make you think ... it's a worry.

Such intensity of feeling and affiliation brought with it a pre-occupation with the Subcontinent, where South Asian values and beliefs are alive and evolving. Participants were aware of the problems and political struggles as well as the excitement about the changes taking place in Bangladesh, Pakistan and the Punjab. Involvement with families on the Subcontinent meant that the children felt deeply concerned about the issues that arose there. P1 was aware that her community would identify and connect with events in Kashmir. To reaffirm their identity, participants would sometimes relate more closely to political and social issues in their country of origin than to events in the UK. For example in their group interviews, C9(P) [sounding earnest and worried] said: 'Miss, India and Pakistan are fighting about Kashmir' and C5 (B) joined in with: 'Why are they fighting over Kashmir?' Their lands of origin affected their sense of security. C6 (P) showed little detachment, he saw Kashmir as his home and described it as: 'Where I live ... ' even though he lived in the UK. But despite the disturbances in their homelands, these pupils felt more secure and confident in their origins than they did in their position as UK citizens, although all but one pupil was born in the UK. Their sense of affiliation with their land of origin and family ties made them concerned about the colonisation of these countries:

C6(P): It used to be West Pakistan and East Pakistan – we used to be ...

C3(B): And there was a fight against Bangladesh and Pakistan.

C6(P): And Miss you know that Pakistan, India and Bangladesh could have been rich ... but ... the English people in the Victorian age, they took all the jewels – took it all.

Cultural and religious knowledge was a priority for these families. The emotional involvement these pupils expressed about their culture and religion could be used to raise pupils' engagement, motivation and achievements. Holt (1996) notes that: 'A child is most intelligent when the reality before him arouses in him [sic] a high degree of attention, interest, concentration, involvement – in short he cares about what he is doing' (p214). Ignoring this body of knowledge devalues the pupils. Writing about a similar situation for the Indigenous children of Australia, Morgan (1995) describes the disappointment the children felt about learning at school: 'She [the teacher] placed my book on my desk, and I couldn't help groaning out aloud. It seemed that Dick, Dora, Nip and Fluff had somehow managed to graduate to Grade Two. In a way, I felt sorry for them. None of them lived near a swamp, and there was no mention of wild birds, snakes or goannas. I resigned myself to another year of boredom' (p23). Curriculum relevance, such as valuing the parents' priority of learning the Koran, will develop links with the parents.

P1 understood that the parents prioritise learning the Koran over learning at school.

P1 was aware of these priorities but believed that the parents felt they lacked the knowledge to be involved in the education provided by the school:

P1:   How do they [Pakistani parents] question something they don't know about?

She identified 'Not a fear but almost a reluctance because they think oh these are all teachers; they know what they are doing and because parents feel 'we don't know". But she thought some parents were involved in school, although only in particular ways:

P1:   At the moment again it's education ... with the recent Ofsted report saying that Pakistani children are way down, right, almost at the bottom and that's quite a priority. And there's maintaining the culture and the religion, keeping the children enclosed within those things. They know the children need be good at Maths English and Science ... the other subjects they don't often, [they] are not too fussed about things like Music or PE, Geography. It's only English, Maths and Science that they think they need to know and that they need to keep up with.

There were pressures on parents to educate their children in both the communities' cultures and the school's. A Pakistani parent conversant with the meanings in the *Koran* or *Guru Gransab* would be able to discuss them more confidently than the National Curriculum. But for the teacher it was the other way round. The school's ignorance of the cultural expectations and concerns of the parents was compounded the poor representation of their concerns among the staff.

Pupils and their priorities

We have seen that the pupils had priorities other than their school careers. The Sikh pupils had more liberal and less routine practices compared with the Muslims. But they expressed concern about being in a minority and relatively isolated:

C11(S): It's like in this school there are lots of Pakistanis and I feel the odd one out.

C10(S) commented on her choice of secondary school:

C10(S):I want to go to ... school ... [where] there's Sikhs ... there's more Sikhs there.

Lack of role models

Certain issues applied to the communities as a whole. The disregard for the cultural knowledge and identity of the communities was evident from the lack of Black teachers in schools that had over seventy percent of Black pupils. The lack of representation meant the school system reinforced the inequality in society. S1 expressed concern that the school did not acknowledge the importance of role models as illustrated in the quote at the beginning of this chapter.

Although the teacher participants in this study were potential role models for South Asian pupils, their positions were severely compromised by the demands of the curriculum, Ofsted and their inadequate connection with the communities.

Parker-Jenkins (1995) argues that British society fails to acknowledge the positive strengths of minority cultures and beliefs and that ethnic minorities are profoundly affected by a sense of exclusion at psychological and sociological levels, and that this sense of exclusion has direct consequences for the teachers' sense of self esteem and identity. Teacher M is well aware of the importance of her pupils' identity and self esteem but is given little opportunity to focus on what matters to them.

Some parents were cynical about the prejudice and stereotyping of South Asian pupils by the teachers, but thought it useless to complain about this institutional racism.

Because of their limited knowledge of the school system the children were seldom supported in translating the communities' values into the school context. And some young people may wish to have a clear separation between home and school (Allred *et al*, 2001). Their responses may not be the same as that of adults, although some pupils in this study who were not yet adolescent endorsed their parents' focus.

Summary of positions and perspectives

The educated community representatives understood the disadvantage South Asian parents were at because they knew so little about the UK educational system, and because of the schools' indifference to educating children about their cultures and religions. They were aware of the ignorance that prevailed in both camps and the conflicts caused. However, parents could also lose the respect of their children because of their ignorance of the educational system. One participant reported that children could be resentful towards their parents, so that the parents were criticised by both the school and their children. Vincent (1992) states that parents often feel excluded from school or a nuisance; they can also feel unhappy because their children at times take more notice of their teachers than of them.

Thus educational policy maintains inequalities in several ways. It fails to monitor or address institutional racism and fails also to integrate the important cultural concerns of the parents that exist outside school.

Although there is legislation which claims to enhance parental control, in practice micropolitical processes maintain institutional power and inhibit parents from developing an independent voice (Vincent, 2001). The school system reinforces the sense of difference and constraint parents experienced in society. And the parents' cultural expectations were framed within a collectivist rather than an individualist paradigm. The notion of a child aiming to attain autonomy and separateness, typified by demanding and assertive toddlers, differs greatly from a view of the watchful and imitative child as respected in South Asian and African cultures (Edwards, 1995), and an interdependent rather than independent style of child-rearing (Levy, 1995). The teacher in the Mosque's positive expectations contrast with the schoolteacher's emphasis on the difficulties and potential learning failures of children, observed by Gregory (1994). Belief in children's success is crucial to their own self-belief and endorses the need for more Black teachers in schools who understand the children's worlds. However, the difference in pedagogy and expectation also suggests a need to synthesise elements from both cultures and enhance cross-cultural learning by combining affective and cognitive styles of teaching and learning.

With the school focus on cognitive skills, staff need to work creatively with cognitive dissonance. Western pedagogy accepts that questioning is a crucial explorative tool, with the potential to open our minds to diversity and challenge our perceptions. But teaching based on one consensual meaning inhibits an awareness of different perspectives, and the strict curriculum content negates the role of questioning (de Rijke and Sinter, 1996). In the redrafting of the National Curriculum certain languages receive more attention than others (Kearney, 1996). The languages and perceptions of non-western cultures are insufficiently integrated into the curriculum. Without comparisons that would offer alternatives, different perspectives cannot be questioned in the way de Rijike and Sinter recommend.

However, the crucial component, the communities themselves, may well have resources to help develop a creative and dynamic awareness of the cross-cultural situation. Deploring the lack of bilingual perspectives in the National Curriculum, Kearney (1996) argues that there are deep unresolved issues of identity and culture to be addressed and calls for 'more research to be conducted with community groups in the British context, to assess needs and aspirations and establish a meaningful dialogue' (p248).

The list below aims to help teachers evaluate their school's relationship with the local communities and the avenues for developing a constructive exchange of knowledge.

Checklist for teachers evaluating their relationship with local communities

- Is the school open and inviting to the communities and if so in what ways?

- Are you able to be proactive about developing links with the communities?

- Are you able to adapt the curriculum?

- Have you adapted parts of the curriculum in response to parents' or the communities' needs and perspectives?

- Do you understand the concerns and priorities of your local communities?

- Can you address any of the above concerns or issues?

- Are there opportunities for you to design and deliver shared curriculum sessions with members of the communities?

- Are there opportunities for parents and community representatives to learn more about the different pedagogic beliefs and practices in the western educational system?

This chapter has shown how cross-cultural struggles and tensions can stimulate awareness and moments of revelation. A state of disequilibrium may elicit a more dynamic and creative response. This possibility is most tangible in the dynamic response, as discussed in the following chapter.

6

The dynamic response

S3: There's all this confusion and fusion ... We've got a new understanding of ourselves: about our identity.

They're [the younger generation] not losing their culture: they're just transforming it and adapting it.

The dynamic response expresses excitement and engagement with change, a perceptual agility that exists despite the constraints imposed in certain contexts. It highlights bicultural skills: a capacity to synthesise and discriminate between different perspectives and experiences. It is characterised by creativity, imagination and the courage to challenge accepted beliefs and practices. It blends a capacity to create a sense of self and retain a sense belonging without compromising independence of mind and initiative. The concept of independence remains in a context of being South Asian, so still part of a collective group. This explains why a person might prefix 'British' with Pakistani, Sikh, Bangladeshi, Muslim etc. Qualities that may be construed as western are not quite the same within this non-western paradigm, although the western emphasis on individualism has been an influence. One way to clarify the difference between an essentially western concept of independence and a South Asian interpretation is to locate the sense of independence within a religious context, such as Sikhism.

Sikhism has dynamic qualities (Ballard, 1994): its origins are political as well as religious. Sikhism was a revolutionary struggle to address the inequalities of the caste system and to synthesise and develop positive elements of both Islam and Hinduism. However, its emphasis on equality creates contradictions and paradoxes: Sikhism combines individualism with communal enterprise. I found a pre-dominance of Sikhs adopting this dynamic response. Freedom of choice is one Sikh ideal and this presents a challenge to conformity as well as the potential to express an independent voice:

S2: Sikhism, it's not very intense – like it's up to the individual how they take their religion. So you'll get the westernised versions of Sikhism – people who will cut their hair and wear the wes-ternised clothes.

S1 and S2 note that Sikh beliefs are focused on the importance of personal choice, and the way both women expressed themselves indicated their sense of autonomy in the decisions they reached. S1 notes how Sikhism's strength is in allowing people to decide for themselves how they will observe Sikhism:

S1: I was never forced into it [Sikhism] that's probably why I've got clearer ideas about what I am doing and where I want to go in terms of religion ... When people actually turn to it then it's going to be because they've actually turned to it – because they actually want to – rather than because they've been indoctrinated.

S1 values the importance of choice in relation to Sikhism, while S3 is impressed with its focus on equality:

S3: Sikhism means something to me because I grew up with this idea that everyone is equal but I believe that there is one religion. There's no difference in the religions of the world.

S3 described Sikhism as a secular religion because she feels it is pos-sible to agree with the sacred tenets of Sikhism without having to observe the religious rituals. Although she was introduced to the rituals as a child, as an adult she has opted to ignore many of them:

S3: It's a secular religion. What I like about Sikhism is that as a child I grew up in a Sikh family ... and we were new in the fifties so we all set up [built] the temple where we used to go all the time and everyone got married there ... So it was a part of my life when I grew up .... So I grew up really in the temple. I was told all these things but I didn't really understand, but as I grew up I learned a bit more about life. And I have a funny relationship with Sikhism because I have the relationship with it as a child and I have another relationship with it as an adult. I do find what it says and what it does is two different things.

The Muslim members of the communities described ways in which the observance of Ramadan focuses on equality and sharing and they too drew attention to ways of resolving paradoxes and tensions and to independence of mind. P1 articulates the need to explore the implications of the contrasting experiences and influences presented by Islam itself:

P1: They [young people] need to grow up feeling confident and proud ... to be able to understand why parents do not let you do this and, you know, find their boundaries ...There's grey areas as well, so they need to explore that.

The radical Pakistani, P3, found her own way of interpreting Islam and offered a different perspective to prayer and fatality from others in her family and the Muslim communities. She stated that she was 'not using God to get good marks ... I mean what's the point, I mean he's going to die now [her brother was dying of cancer] so what's the use of praying. The only reason I'd pray was not to make him better but ... take him away more quickly ... to ease the pain'. This was a quite different attitude from the rest of the family's and P3 felt free to develop her own interpretations of life and Islam, and her family accepted this.

The religious paradigm clarifies some difference from western individualism but it accounts for only one aspect of being South Asian in the UK. P3's assertion of being different from others in her community is combined with attachment to family, community and the sense of belonging identified in the reaffirming response. So various elements converge to influence the cross-cultural experience of South Asian community members. As P3 describes, circumstance alone, unconnected with religion, creates tensions and disjunctures which demand resolution. Rassool (1999) argues that immigrant pupils experience an 'ongoing process of critique, evaluation, negotiation, self affirmation and validation of themselves in relation to their particular experiences in everyday life' (p28). The sense of dynamic and movement she identifies is similar to that expressed by the participants in this study but these participants were not just schoolchildren but mothers and community representatives too.

This pursuit of alternative self-definition, which synthesises contrasting cultural beliefs and values, is essential to the survival of South Asian identity both in the UK and at global level. It is vital for South Asian people to develop their own modernism. In his book *The Present History of West Bengal*, Chatterjee (1997) draws attention to the debilitating impact of colonialism on Indian self-identity and progress and suggests that modernity that has been established by others must be rejected. He writes:

> Modernity for us is like a supermarket of foreign goods, displayed on the shelves: pay up and take away what you like. No one there [in the West] believes that we could be producers of modernity ... Ours is the modernity of the once-colonised. The same, historical process that has taught us the value of modernity has also made us the victims of modernity (p210).

Chatterjee stresses the need for the insider's perspective and ability to recreate identity and culture, which demands certain skills and qualities.

The dynamic response captures processes of evaluation and critique. It to some degree recreates identity and culture in the way Chatterjee asserts is essential. The characteristics and skills expressed in this response can resolve certain of the disjunctures experienced at a perceptual level. Young South Asian women are involved in constant negotiations. As Basit (1997) puts it: 'I want more freedom but not too much'. This dynamic was found among parents and community elders, not only among the young nor just within a school context, but also within the heart of diverse South Asian communities where several different perspectives prevailed.

Circumstances and contexts, however, can inhibit this perceptual flexibility. S1 emphasised how the concept of freedom in the West 'lures' one, while pupil C9 (P) suggested that Pakistan is a 'free country'. Here we see tension between concepts and contexts. The freedom C9(P) is talking about is to do with living in a context where parents are more relaxed than in the UK, feel a sense of belonging and do not fear loosing their traditional beliefs. By contrast, 'freedom' as a Western concept implies negotiable limitations, a sense of abandonment, and knows no boundaries. Despite the conceptual and cultural tools developed by participants, tensions that exist in the school, as described in the contradictory and constrained response, are not necessarily resolved. For instance institutional racism and racism in society still constrain people. So although members of the communities may offer a more imaginative response in this chapter, they cannot themselves overcome racism:

S3:   I'd rather not live here – I'd rather go and live in the country like in Dorset or Cornwall. That's what I want to do but I can't just go and live anywhere when there's racial prejudice and I've got two Asian girls to bring up. That's why I live here. That's why I'll always live in the inner city in a multicultural area.

Although the interviewees managed to find some kind of resolution to these problems, the ways were not dynamic. S2 commented that 'we do come across a lot more racism' [comparing it to another part of the UK where she had lived]. However, she understood that the location of an inner city area in itself created problems particular to the city:

S2:   Maybe ... living in this area ... [there are] kids on the street and obviously there's drugs and everything around. I want my kids not to be anywhere near that type of environment.

S2 said she had thought about these problems frequently, and could disentangle the roots of certain of her experiences of racism. P2 expressed his pain and disorientation when subjected to racism, but had come to understand that 'It's just the way it is – you learn to accept it'. This implies some resolution, but hardly represents a dynamic response, only a kind of acceptance. Although his response is similar to the avoidance identified in the reaffirming response, there was a more conscious recognition of avoidance as a strategy and thus a more empowering way of resolving the difficulty. S3 recognised the limitations of her identity and was realistic about racism. Her knowledge of racism in society, and her pride in her Asian origins made living in this inner city environment acceptable, if not ideal.

The realities of institutional racism in schools, the exclusionary curriculum and the low expectations held by teachers, along with the communities' relative ignorance about the educational system, cannot be resolved by one individual's thoughtfulness and imagination. The dynamic response is to some degree context based. Certain opportunities allow it to flourish.

Although the responses are by their nature dynamic and based upon interaction and contexts, the term dynamic as applied here conveys a catalyst for change: a conscious, critical perspective and the ability to cope with the social and cognitive struggles implicit in cross-cultural situations. The dynamic response is characterised by a process of development, and qualities like openness, broadmindedness and social flexibility. The skills entailed are complex and require conceptual dexterity; evaluation and reflectivity; independence of mind; emotional security; courage to think again and re-evaluate deeply held attachments and affiliations. Creativity and imagination culminate in a synthesis of beliefs and values emanating from a range of sources and experiences. This synthesis retains essential qualities that are identifiably South Asian but the beliefs and values are not constrained by the past. This response has the potential to bring about change on a wider scale.

Openness, broadmindedness and social flexibility

A crucial factor in generational differences in responses is the flexibility of the younger generation in their use of language, whereas the members of the communities had to make a conscious decision to broaden their perspectives and to recognise the opportunities for development. P3, who is in her mid twenties, understood that her community needed to be more broad-minded and to mix in the outside world. She was well aware of prejudice and of the barriers her own community sets up against other cultural groups and also against women. She was glad that other independent individuals in the community stood up for themselves. She considered that for children to become successful they would need:

P3: A good education and being able to socialise with other ethnic minorities – not just their own kind. Because I've noticed most Pakistani girls tend to stick to their own kind and I don't like that.

She recognised the importance of 'being able to mix with other ethnic minorities [in school]. The Mosque can't do that. There you're there with your own kind ... it could be seen as racism'. Her eagerness to be more adventurous, broadminded and expansive about identity was also apparent among some parents and community representatives. S3 clearly asserts her complex identity:

S3: First thing I would like to say is that I am an Indian and also that as far as my religion is concerned I'm Sikh ... There's a lot of identities about being an Indian. The fact that my skin is brown and the fact that I've been born in Britain and then there's the culture and then there's my relationship with Britain because I am a Black person in Britain so there's lots of relationships to India. And part of being a Sikh is that it is just one of many religions in India.

This complexity is enriched in the multicultural environment in which these South Asian communities are located and which can itself engender broadmindedness, as P2 observes:

P2: You have to be broadminded, I mean you have to be aware because the Asian community doesn't just consist of Muslims, it consists of other Indians: Sikhs, Bangladeshis, Sri Lankans even. Although we speak more or less the same language – we've got the same sort of similar values. To me my community is not just the Muslim community or the Pakistani – I respect all – as well as the English and Black community. We have to try to work together – but it doesn't always work.

The South Asian pupils also expressed a desire to move on and open up to situations that might have been contentious in the past. Although they knew about the colonial exploitation of India, some were eager to move to a conciliatory response:

C5(B): But England's people ... forgot about it ... they're friends now ... Cos there's no point, there's no point um fighting about it now, cos it's gone already now ...

SCG: You get on with them?

C5(B): Yeah.

SCG: With English people?

C3(B): Yeah.

C5(B) and C3(B) were positive that it was time to move on. They were eager to mention the neighbours or other contacts outside their community with whom they engaged:

C5(B): I got a neighbour; she's really kind, she gives us flowers loads of time. She's really kind. Because – while she was on holiday – we gave her waste – what do you call it ... the dustbin men um he cleaned it – because we look after her dustbin – she gave us a flower once ... .She's an English person.

C3(B): In my house; my dad used to have this friend called Martin who was Jamaican or Somalian or something ... every week he used to get us chocolate and his wife used to bring us these presents.

The multicultural area where these pupils lived presented opportunities to learn about other cultures and to extend understanding. We noted how Teacher M took advantage of any opportunity she was given to integrate the children's diverse backgrounds into the curriculum to make it relevant, and this was appreciated by some parents, including S3.

S3: I want my children to have an all-rounded education and no prejudice. I'd also like them to learn and they do – about different cultures and religions. And she [her daughter] knows about all that because she learnt about that earlier in the year. They were taught about the Caribbean and about Islam.

Sikhism, with its broadmindedness and sense of revelation, allowed S1 and S2 to mix freely with whomever they chose, and S1 found her own connections with other communities. For instance, as a nurse she had observed that white working class people could also have extended families that are wary of outsiders:

S1:   She [a health visitor friend] often talks of the fact that they've got their grandparents who tell them about bottle-feeding and breast-feeding. The health visitor is like an intruder; everyone relies heavily on their extended family.

S1 was interested in what she saw as important links between her culture and that of others. But this was not just because of her Sikhism. Both S3 and P2 recommend openness to others without expressing an affinity with any particular cultural group. Furthermore, as Sikh pupils were invariably a minority, within a minority they often had friends from different backgrounds and cultures:

SCG: Are your friends Sikhs as well?

C10(S):No: They're almost all English.

Such broadmindedness and social flexibility was also expressed in pupils' attitudes towards school. Although all the South Asian pupils expressed strong identification with their home upbringing and its priorities, they also expressed a desire to accommodate the requirements of school too. All those interviewed were clear for instance about what they felt were the priorities for their teacher. When asked what their teacher might want or be pleased with, they listed a range of things: 'Doing the correct thing'; 'When you're doing good work and trying hard and not talking that much ... work, behaviour and things ... your knowledge ... our understanding'. And when asked what their teacher helps them with, they replied 'Understand ... how to learn more stuff ... like your history and your English – like if you need to write a letter; then you need good words. And good punctuation ... Good spelling ... Presentation ... And you need to find out more ... And then you've got to take your SATs tests and you've got to prepare that, you've got to prepare for that for two terms.'

Interestingly, they noted their teacher's encouragement of their ability to learn things by heart, as some of them did in the Mosque:

C7(P):   She wants to know if we can learn things by heart. That's why in the afternoon some people read poems.

C8(P):   Reading suras is like that...

SCG: So it's the same as reading the suras?

C7(P):   Yes it's just like that but different.

A few Muslim pupils felt there was a link between their mother and their teacher because both were involved in teaching them:

C2(B):   No actually she's [the teacher] like my mum cos ... she teaches you stuff .

C1(B): She [mother] teaches you stories, my mum told me stories about being a Muslim; about Islam and all that.

These pupils were also very aware of the different expectations held by the school and the Mosque and welcomed the opportunity to try and find links between the two. Apparently everything was translated in relation to their religious beliefs and practices, rather than the other way round. Belief and pride combined to produce a predominantly South Asian perspective, although they were open-minded towards the different values and beliefs held by others. C1(B) identified a link between the Mosque and school when you prayed in the Mosque that you would be good at both. Prayer thus created a sense of importance for both institutions:

C1(B) Actually they're the same; school work and thingy [SATs and also the Mosque teaching] because you have to pray and pray to be good at school.

The pupils understood that the primary difference between themselves and their teacher was to do with religion and they seemed to respect this difference:

SCG: Any difference between the teacher and parents?

C4(B): She's got a different meaning to us.

C1(B): Miss, Miss doesn't believe in anything, like she doesn't go to the temple now.

Although pupils expressed great loyalty to the educational systems in their lands of origin, they respected the gentler approach of their teacher at school:

C5(B): You know in this country teachers they're not that cruel or anything like that; they're kind of kinder.

This comment indicates a certain degree of detachment despite the strong sense of loyalty. It was noticeable that the pupils felt a sense of responsibility and respect for both their teacher and their parents. But they showed deeper loyalty and affinity to their cultural and religious roots and identification with their communities than with the school. The Mosque related to the way they will live their lives and also the meaning of their life. Their eagerness to discuss their cultural values and beliefs in the group interview sessions at the school indicated their desire to integrate both systems and to incorporate more of their cultural meanings and particular identity into the school system.

Many of the Bangladeshi and Pakistani pupils were skilled and confident about their bilingual abilities. This was a typical comment:

C1(B): Sometimes I will speak English and sometimes I will speak Bengali.

Learning languages appeared to be the link between home and Mosque. Language had a symbolic value as a passport to the Subcontinent. Hindi and Urdu programmes are constantly on British TV. The bicultural and sometimes multilingual circumstances and requirements the pupils engaged in made them synthesise a range of skills and knowledge:

C3(B): I can speak Hindi proper. I watch a lot of Hindi films ...

C5(B): Ah we've got a Pakistani – we've got a digital – so we've got a Pakistani channel and it's Arabic.

SCG: Do you learn Urdu in the Mosque?

C10(P): Yes.

C5(B): I read Bengali – cos we've got this Bengali class.

C10(P): I read Arabic.

Their readiness to adjust to whichever contexts suggests the pupils' self-confidence, possibly based on their clear sense of identity. The children expressed clarity about and confidence in their religious identity. Although they were aware of the school's rules, they realised there were far more rules in the Mosque and seemed paradoxically to revere the harsher commitment expected in the Mosque and thought the stricter practices in Pakistan or Bangladesh could be effective:

C7(P): It's a lot easier than Pakistan ... cos [in] Pakistan they have to read Urdu ... plus they don't have playtimes and when they come in the morning and when the teacher's not here, they just play and the teacher says to come back to the classroom and they just come back ... they're more strict about learning.

They seemed impressed by this strictness and the hard work demanded:

C2(B): I heard that the GCSEs in Bangladesh are harder than in England ... They do three subjects – English, Bengali and Arabic and then they have a test on all three of them.

Homework seemed less like homework in Bangladesh. As C5 (B) put it: 'It's not like work, but we always, my cousins, we always read every day at home and in the night cos it's better to learn.'

The pupils' respect for this system seemed to connect with a sense of identification with it. It was tied to *their* world and knowledge. Pride in being South Asian should not be underestimated. Although school was less demanding than the effort and endurance required to learn the Koran and keep to the daily practices, pupils showed loyalty and dedication to their practices.

It could be that racism is an inadvertent catalyst to evolving a complex identity in which having a non-western identity is more reassuring and something to be proud of. The combination of experience of racism and rejection and enthusiasm for being South Asian, broadmindedness and social flexibility can produce something far more impressive than a defensive rejection of western values. There is another kind of identity that Castells (1997) calls *projected identities*. These deal with the need to have a new and more progressive identity – he cites feminism as an example. Castells argues that resistance identity is invariably a reaction against materialism and a refuge, often manifest in religious belief, against a hostile world. And projected identity has the potential to reconstruct national identity. Castells is interested in the need for meaning in our lives that is created through identity and ethnicity. He identifies how communes of resistance defend their space, their places. He articulates the importance of development from resistance, which can be constraining and conservative, however valid, to more liberating projected identities. The capacity to develop a liberating dimension requires social and cognitive skills as well as emotional security. It has to challenge the communities' more conservative elements as well as the prejudices in wider society. S3 puts it simply:

S3:   I don't like the people that I've noticed that are Born Again Christians that say Jesus is alive and then the next day say it's the ten commandments and those that insist on the existence of Allah. So I find it all a bit oppressive whether it's English or whether it's fundamentalist Muslims. So I think the challenge for the community is not to get lost up its own bum in terms of being reactionary.

In these interviews, both pupils and the adult participants show the potential to reach beyond the boundaries of their South Asian communities and enthusiasm for seeing links to the host society. But openness, broadmindedness and social flexibility are not enough in themselves: cognitive skills, such as conceptual dexterity, evaluation and reflexivity are equally vital.

Conceptual dexterity: evaluation and reflectivity

S3 sees faults in both western and South Asian communities. She offers a critical eye:

S3:   No it's not language ... it's this notion of colonisation because most middle-class Asians speak English as a second language. So if they were in schools they could speak English to the teachers. So it's not about language because there's Punjabi speaking teachers in the school. I mean it's about interest – they're not interested. They see the secular world as a material world and they're just there to get as much as they can out of it. So they're really glad that the kids are going to school. And it's secular – if it was religious – if it started to interfere with the religious side of it – then they'd all be there and language wouldn't stop them.

In her opinion, it is the South Asian communities' cultural ignorance and lack of respect for the customs and beliefs of secular society that inhibit communication and understanding between the school and society, and the community and she distanced herself from this outlook. She thinks it fair to be critical of the limitations of South Asian communities, but does not think they should be seen as an alien group. Accordingly, she condemns the perceptions by outsiders of the communities as 'exotic/alien/pariahs' when they do not understand them. She thinks we should recognise that every community has its problems:

S3:   I don't think people in Britain should get lost and think ooh [referring to instances of abuse] that's the culture we'd better leave that alone, that's how people think and that's how they [the communities] live ... [they should understand that] ... It's because they're [community members] not educated themselves ... It's wrong to look at them [South Asians] as if they're these people that have this incurable disease ... A lot of white people don't get involved with their children's education.

Importantly, S3 opted to remove herself from the communities' centres and declined taking on the responsibility of community spokesperson. She could thus avoid having to find a compromise between the different views expressed by those who mixed in the centres, as P1 had to do. So being independent, even an outsider, allows this perspective to flourish. Such independence demands self-evaluative skills, and S3 was able to be critically analytical and objective about her own upbringing and the influences in her life. She recognised how she had changed her views over time in response to the sophisticated and complex understanding her education and geographical mobility had allowed her to develop. She would not want her own children to be brought up as she was.

> S3: I found my upbringing really oppressive. I have the impression that they [the community in this study] are like the community I grew up in. I know that's quite a limited view because I don't know them but I suppose the contact I do have means that I recognise the community and I was quite shocked when I saw this. Here they're just living with the old village traditions especially about women ... my feeling is that it's going to have to change. I think it's probably *the women that are changing inside themselves and that it's the girls who are making those changes*; it's just important that they don't hide it. [my emphasis]

The words in italics suggest some self-awareness, which S3 has also identified in other women. She is aware of the limitations of the local community and can explain why they are trapped in the past and show a sense of inferiority and some ignorance. However, her separateness from the communities might influence her to underestimate the social and emotional skills that several of the parents expressed. P2 had found his own way of dealing with the cultural clashes experienced by South Asian parents but mixed regularly with his community:

> P2: We do get lecturers regularly at the religious centres that you have to understand our children today because there's a culture clash. I think you need more understanding and you can't just scream and shout and say you have to do this; you have to do that. You only understand anything is when you are told quietly; calmly ... because we are in a modern society we're not in an Islamic state or anything. This is an English country.

P2 recognised his views were unusual, but he observed changes happening around him and had initiated changes in his own home set-up to adjust to living in a cross-cultural situation. Many parents worked hard to integrate the beliefs and knowledge of their religious and cultural origins into society. S3 offered her children insight into their Sikh culture and language, taking them to the Gurdwaras and giving them creative lessons in Punjabi. She would like her daughter to learn Hindi as well:

> S3: She [her daughter] has a story book and I teach her ... and sometimes we read stories or make them up and give them an idea of the vocabulary as well ... I've been trying to get my husband to teach her some Hindi.

S1 prioritises schoolwork over religious instruction at times.

S1:   Although I may want to sit and read the *Granthsab* for fifteen minutes or so, I won't force them to come and sit down with me. But I will force them to do their homework.

The ways of resolving difference presented so far in the dynamic response demonstrate the ability to mix in more than one cultural group, to empathise with the experiences of others and the skill to determine which aspects of South Asian cultural practices and ideals to identify with. Although the participants recognised the West's sense of freedom and equality, they still considered it preferable to translate western ideas into a South Asian version rather than to adopt western ideals unquestioningly. Moreover, the reality of racism prevented anyone from feeling unquestioning attachment to the UK.

S3 is aware of the complexity and multiplicity of identities and seeks a combination of beliefs and interests of her own. This explorative approach led her to the ancient pagan elements in the Hindu religion surrounding ideas about the goddess Kali. She recognised the strengths and weaknesses in both western and eastern beliefs but preferred the depths of eastern beliefs and found western ideas shallow by comparison. S3, like P2, P1 and others, was thus open and interested in differences but found ways to meld them into their own perspective. It was a perspective that combined evaluation with reflexivity and openness.

The quandary about what to keep and what to discard in their background and culture tests the cognitive, social and affective skills of South Asians in the West. Paradoxes and confusions have to be resolved. Members of the South Asian communities are challenged to become bicultural in a way that people exposed only to western values may not have to confront. The South Asian participants had to reflect not only upon their ways of life and their beliefs but also on why they wished to maintain a South Asian identity when they chose to integrate alternative values, and on how to do so. S3 articulates how this involves discriminating between emotional and cognitive needs: ' ... I mean there's a lot of rubbish in the culture ... it's all got to be thrown away'. And on another instance she notes that ' ... You want to keep that love and that closeness ... '

This collision of differences, of old ideas and new, presented an endless challenge for the communities. Although some members focused on preserving certain aspects of their culture that others were less interested in, there was one area about which all were unanimous. All considered it vital for their children to visit the Sub-continent. Even S3, the most radical of all the people interviewed, believed this:

S3: I'd like them to see their relatives and the Punjab and I'd probably take them to a Gurdwara and one or two temples ... [and visit Orissa] I mean you go back to the temple and you're always in the temple – because it's part of the life there ... I know people who went in their childhood and it really transformed them ... And people who never went did feel the gap ... I'd love to go back and see the house and place.

S3's experience of the Punjab and India did not, however, make things easier for her on a conceptual level. Her visits also made her aware that the community she lived in was similar to the communities she'd encountered on the Subcontinent. So although her visit to her land of origin was pleasurable and emotionally reassuring, she sought to move away from the parts of the culture that she considered rigid or restrictive. This meant she had to evolve her own approach to child rearing. She would rather her daughters had greater choice than the children she saw on the Subcontinent, and a wider range of options and understandings open to them. Whether they become Sikh or not is not of prime importance to her. She anticipates that her children will synthesise their cultural heritage with contemporary values in the UK and develop their own minds.

S3: My priorities, well ... are that they [her children] should learn social skills and that they should learn to start living with each other in like a civilised way and that they should have an academic education and also that their creativity should be nurtured and their spirituality and not in an orthodox way ... I don't know. I mean as far as religion is concerned, we never say there isn't a God but then we don't say God is anything in particular, so we do let her be ... I don't know if our children will be Sikh, I think they'll make up their own mind.

Independence of mind plus emotional security

All the interviewees who developed alternative perspectives and understandings of their cross-cultural situation demonstrated clearly that independence of mind was essential. But independence alone was acknowledged to be isolating and considered selfish so not at all desirable. But it demanded respect for the relative freedom allowed by parents or community representatives. In other words, independence was linked to a sense of social belonging and this in turn ensured emotional security. This attachment and sense of belonging was clearer among other South Asian participants than S3.

Independence was exemplified by P3, and at first I found no ties or attachments beneath it. She was proud of her independence and initiative as a student who had gained a degree against the odds. She spoke about the courage required to be different in a context where individualism can be scorned. She made clear her dislike of the insular nature of the community and made no pretence about its prejudices. She held a special position, as someone to whom the young people turned for understanding, despite the tensions this could create. P3 felt that she could offer her young relatives positive ideas and she ignored the limitations of her Elders on certain issues: 'Most of my cousins come to me for advice. But I don't think their parents like it'.

P3 wished to offer her younger relatives a greater sense of freedom. Although she respected her Elders and certain of the traditions, she thought that some of the rules were unnecessarily rigid and left the younger generation unheard and repressed:

P3:   When you're younger you're invited to parties and things ... and you do want to go ... but your parents will say no ... you shouldn't be mixing and that you will end up eating something you shouldn't ... and then you have to cover up your disappointment.

Hutnik (1991) and Modood (1994) suggest that affirming a South Asian identity does not necessarily indicate that the person will adopt the traditional cultural practices. It is important to examine how affiliation to a South Asian identity may also be manifest in non-South-Asian ways – a complex response which has emerged over the last two decades. P3 felt confident enough to forge a different way ahead for herself despite community pressures:

P3:   Well for me I was just very interested in education but there was no one there for me, to help me – I just had to do it all myself ... I'm the odd one out – I don't know why? ... I was student of the year at my college and everyone was shocked because I'm pretty shy and I got [this recognition] that for two years and I go to Uni ... women can do it on their own as well and can be independent.

She felt that the Muslim community was not really interested in women's education but she was determined not to become a housewife:

SCG: You're not going to be a housewife?

P3:   No way.

So P3 was able to take an independent approach and recognise that this can work. She still retained a loyalty for her own community, however, despite their insularity. The layers to her identity and security could be played out at different times. She believed her family provided her ultimate sense of security.

There were other instances of enlightened community groups, which took a more broadminded approach to South Asian values and beliefs than the norm. P1, for example, cites the women who attend her centre:

P1:   The women want to know more, want to learn more ... They said: we want jobs; we want to learn – there's nowhere we can go – where do we go? We want to learn training; we want to learn computing, we want to learn, to do courses, we want to better ourselves so that we can get out there.

Ultimately the decision to take a new stance depended upon courage, independence of mind and most importantly, a sense of belonging too. So to use independence of mind as a western concept that has influenced non-western people is not completely accurate. The individualism or independence expressed by P3 or S3 encompasses their sense of belonging to a group, sharing an identity with South Asians or being closely linked to family and, on occasion, community identity.

However, creativity and imagination bring a further dimension to the ability to step outside and take a different stance and it is this dimension which is most innovative and ultimately sustaining.

Creativity and synthesis

Despite or possibly at times because of the challenges presented by living in culturally different UK context, members of the communities had developed their creativity, synthesising a complex range of beliefs and values. Hall (1990) describes the way in which displaced cultural groups and cultural minorities can have a fragmented self-identity, disorientated by their historical experience. Although he is writing about African-Americans, the categories he develops are helpful for understanding the contradictory elements of minorities living in the UK. He coins the term 'diaspora identity':

Diaspora identities are those which are constantly producing and reproducing themselves anew, through transformation and difference' (Hall, 1990: 235). He stresses the mobile process of developing cultural identities: '[Cultural identities] come from somewhere, have histories. But like everything else, which is historical, they undergo constant transformation. Far from being externally fixed in some essentialist past, they are subject to continuous 'play' of history, culture and power ... cultural identity is a matter of 'becoming' as well as of 'being'. It belongs to the future as much as to the past. (p394)

If culture is 'on the move', the same will be true of identities: for example, S3 is inspired by the idea that identity can be about colour and not just about religion:

S3:   That's a new form of identity ... to say that your identity relates to your skin colour. And I find that exciting because I met a native American ... there was just so much excitement about meeting, just based on the brown skin.

S3 was excited and challenged rather than threatened by realising that there are different and dynamic ways of dealing with difference and cross-cultural conflict. She was open to exploring possibilities and creatively synthesising a range of perspectives and experiences:

S3:   And I think the culture is evolving anyway. I mean I think the other part of westernization is that the colonisation is finished. I think it's becoming glaringly obvious to people who come from world-wide origin that even if their culture has been disparaged that it's not true. And I feel that all the cultures that colonialism touched – which is basically all the world – is that the younger generation are beginning to pick and choose and discriminate between what they want to keep and what they don't. And they realise that with music and the media they're not losing their culture, they're just transforming it and adapting it. And I feel the strength of my own family and my Indian culture because everyone's changed; I mean I've seen changes that I would have never dreamt would have happened ... I imagined that people would marry English people and get divorced and eat roast beef and potatoes on Sunday but it's not happened.

S3 saw change as inevitable and saw how it clears away the most constraining elements in the culture – especially the prejudice in the communities towards women, and how this was now being addressed:

S3:   Lots of feminist women I know who left home at seventeen or had to lie and who were called sluts and things like that; I mean now a lot of them want to go to the Gurdwara and pray and we're saying it's our temple – it's ours, and it believes in equality as well and we are not going to tolerate you shitty patriarchs. You know

> I think there's going to be a real shift in who actually is going to take ownership of the culture ... And people are doing it in India and people are sending the old crotchety mother-in-laws – who say stay at home and do the cooking; they're sending them to psychiatrists. I mean there's a lot of rubbish in the culture ... it's all got to be thrown away.

Note that part of S3's ability to be dynamic was due to her uncompromising and extreme position. She was not prepared to compromise or allow herself to be confused for long. But she is positive about the creative strengths of mixing western and eastern cultures, while recognising that there is much to discover or rediscover about eastern cultures.

S3:   With the western culture there's this confusion and fusion. I think it's just going to go on blending, ending and evolving. But the thing is, the more you do that, the more people go back to their own culture ... digging more out. There's this kind of treasure chest of knowledge, craft and art and religion and spirituality and it's pouring into eastern music nowadays ... you've got sort of *qawwali* [Sufi poetry evoking a trance-like state through voice and tabla] and Hindu chants – so they're mixing all the religions and I think there's a lot of hope there. Because there was a time when they were strict with all the younger generations and saying I'm Muslim, I'm Sikh, I'm this and they're not doing that in the music and the culture. And there's all this older generation ... people who grew up in the sixties and seventies ... and they're all very progressive with the younger generation.

S3 knows precisely what she would like to preserve of her cultural inheritance and what aspects of the West she finds unappealing and unhelpful. She describes her growing awareness of the positive elements of South Asian culture and its importance:

S3:   You want to keep that love and that closeness and kindness for each other. Because I think there was a lot more understanding [interest in] ... English families and people used to look up to [them]. But now we're finding that they don't look after their parents, and brothers and sisters don't love each other. And parents just because they have love marriages; it doesn't mean they love each other more than arranged marriages love each other. So we've got a new understanding of ourselves about our identity that we are going to survive.

Her confidence about being South Asian and belonging to the community was based on ideas and beliefs she had considered carefully, not on loyalty and obedience.

S3 and others express a range of cognitive and social skills, many of which relate to Byram's model of bicultural development. Their skills informed the developmental model outlined in chapter two. For example the broadmindedness and openness combined with social flexibility relate to Byram's concepts of openness and ability to decentre. Independence of mind along with emotional security as illustrated in this chapter relate to role model characteristics and also to Byram's creative integration of knowledge. Such creativity is enhanced by an ability to understand and deal with disjuncture and dissonance.

Suggested classroom sessions and activities relating to the dynamic response

Sessions 5 and 6 analyse and summarise what has been learned, evaluate what has been most enjoyable and interesting and then move on to thinking about resolutions, paradoxes and creative possibilities. This chapter has considered creative dissonance, synthesis and transformation of knowledge, and these are reflected in the sessions. So they are concerned with:

■ evaluating learning, stepping back and reflecting on what has been learned from others, integrating different perspectives, and

■ recognising dissonance, contrast and creative possibilities. Producing a piece of art

The sessions aim to

■ draw on material from the previous sessions and integrate knowledge on identity, cultural diversity, difference, racism, role models and conflict resolution and find ways of viewing controversy and disjuncture

■ work creatively to synthesise and augment the understanding of diversity

■ develop the children's knowledge and understanding of cultures

■ recognise the importance of our collective and individual sense of self by remembering what was learnt in sessions two and three about similarities and differences and the importance of self belief and a sense of belonging

- offer experience of solving problems in a group by means of discussion, debate or through the creative arts
- develop flexible thinking in pupils by asking them to write a story or draw a picture describing a day in the life of person from a culture different from their own

Below are some inspiring quotes for teachers and children, which link back to the earlier sessions and facilitating understanding and creativity. They come from *Here, There and Everywhere* (Richardson, 2005).

■ Local and global vision:

Beyond their world
Beyond their garden in summer were fields of wheat and barley and oats, which sighed and rustled and filled the air with sleepy pollen and earth scents. These fields were large and flat,

And stretched away to a distant line of trees set in the hedgerows.

To the children at that time these trees marked the boundary of their world.

Beyond their world enclosed by the trees there was, they were told, a wider world, with other hamlets and villages and towns and the sea and, beyond that, other countries, where people spoke languages different from their own. Their father had told them so.

But they had no mental picture of these, they were but ideas, unrealised: whereas in their own little world within the tree boundary everything appeared to them more than life-size, and more richly coloured. (Flora Thompson, about life in an English village in the 1880s.)

■ Balancing contrasting perceptions of history:

Where was the balance?
I remember the excitement with which I greeted the amazing new world of my secondary school – a place to conquer life's mysteries and storm through the broad corridors of adolescence.

Reality was a little different, however. My newfound world was a singularly white, all boys grammar school where the National Front [now it would be the BNP] would be happily distributing leaflets at our school gates and an embittered music teacher would ritualistically prod me out of the music rooms for attempting Indian ragas without a written score. Indian classical music is an oral tradition. I never had the heart to break it to him. So what was I taught? History. Yes, I was taught history. How wonderful an experience it would be, I imagined, to learn the origins of my ancestors – to learn of the Aryan journey to the Indus valley and of the Dravidians' historic migration to south India. How inspiring to hear of the great Mogul empire and origins of the Vedas, the

Upanishads and the epic Maharabharata, I thought. What I did learn however was a lot easier to grasp than any of that. Five words: 'India was a British colony.' I had no problem with what I was taught per se ... But where was the balance? Where was I in this ambitious picture of world history?

So I went through school with an uneasy suspicion that I was inferior. It may have been a product of the notion that the history of the non-white population of this world is embedded in slavery and colonisation, or perhaps the echoing resonance of the word Paki as it accompanied me through the hostile corridors of the science block.

Still, in school where the subject of history meant 'History of the White men' and music revolved around Western classical harmony and counterpoint, I guess I emerged fairly well balanced ... (Nitin Sawney, 2003)

■ Surviving racism:

We here
Extracts from a sermon preached to slaves in nineteenth century America
Here, in this here place we flesh; flesh that weeps, laughs; flesh that dances on bare grass. Love it. Love it hard. Yonder they do not love your flesh. They despise it. They don't love your eyes; they'd just as soon pick em out. Nor do they love the skin on your back. Yonder they flay it. And O my people they do not love your hands. Those they only use, tie, bind, chop off and leave empty. Love your hands. Love them! Love them. Raise them up and kiss them. Touch others with them, pat them together, stroke them on your face cos they don't love that either. You got to love it, you!

And no, they ain't in love with your mouth. Yonder, out there, they will see it broken and break it again. What you say out of it they will not heed. What you scream from it they do not hear. What you put into it to nourish your body they will snatch away and give you leavins instead. No, they don't love your mouth. *You* got to love it ... (*Beloved*, by Toni Morrison, 1987)

As with the previous sessions it is vital to have facilitators from a number of cultures working in the sessions so they can make contributions about their own cultures and act as role models.

Session 5

Evaluation is central to this session, returning to the previous sessions and drawing out what the children have felt, thought and learned so far. Children may need to reminded of the earlier sessions. One way to make the evaluation less obvious is to use the symbols of hearts, diamonds, spades and clubs as follows.

- Hearts = your feelings?
- Diamonds = hard facts/knowledge?
- Spades = what question has it raised/reflections?
- Clubs (lucky clover) = what was special/what did you enjoy about the sessions?

Ask the children how they might present some of the ideas to an assembly or to another class. Invite them to design their own session – what would they focus on?

In preparation for Session 6 they can start to write a poem, a rap tune or piece of music or drama that expresses some of the questions and uncertainties the sessions have raised. Alternatively their creative possibilities can be used to design a self portrait, portrait of the local communities or other positively affirming elements.

Session 6
Being creative with dissonance: New beginnings

Contrasting images: Modern Art such as paintings by Francis Bacon or Pablo Picasso can be compared with pictures of the Indian gods, Buddhist paintings or Mogul art. Also art by South African artists, for example 'M K' Malefane's picture of Nelson Mandela (in *Art of the South African Townships* by Gavin Younge) can be analysed for its message. Aboriginal art can be linked to the pointillism of the impressionists. The free expression that characterised some can be juxtaposed with the use of mantras and rituals that express order and predictable form.

Activity: As S3 suggested, the meaning of the Hindu goddess Kali introduces a challenge to Christian or Islamic understanding of meanings. Unlike in Christianity and Islam, the Hindu gods portray diverse elements in life and the goddess Kali presents, among other things, the existence of argument. This could be used to introduce discussion about conflict and power, linking back to session three. The children can draw pictures of good and evil, war and peace, or alternatively of their role model. Collages and mixed media can be an effective way of including images from the media, adapting or transforming them. The 'art landscape' session in chapter seven is also relevant here.

Activity: Aboriginal paintings draw attention to meanings, craft and art as a form of creative communication. Use a selection of books on Aboriginal Art, a recording of Aboriginal story telling from the

'Dreaming' – describing the origins of the land. You will need match-sticks, paper, colours made with thick powder paint, and a CD of world music. Start the activity by listening to a story from the 'Dreaming'. The children then work in groups to discuss their own story and adventure. Show them Aboriginal dot paintings and ask them to work out what they think the symbols and dots in the pictures mean. Then ask them to explain the importance of being patient and meticulous to get the effect required. Finally, they design their own dot painting, while world music is played in the background.

Bangra verses, rap tunes, poetry and prose can all inspire children. Community members from Africa or the Subcontinent can introduce the art and concepts from their own countries, as suggested the sessions in chapter seven. Most importantly, the value of oral cultures is best explained by people from countries where it dominates, such as Somalia. Songs sung to introduce a poem, story or song (like 'Crick-crack; break my back') can be used as the beginning and ending to performances.

An opportunity must be provided for childen to express their feelings and transform the experiences and issues debated, by writing a poem or song, drawing a picture and doing something creatively as a group: designing a poster, writing a leaflet or arranging a freeze, and celebrating the work by presenting an assembly for the rest of the school to enjoy.

Sources: Richardson (2005) suggests using: Journey stories compiled through interviews and constructing pieces of prose which tell the stories of people in different lands in English lessons, or presenting traditional folktales to engage discussion and argument about important issues in the school using shadow puppets.

For Music, inventing the story of an encounter between two or more cultures can be told in sound.

The Runnymede Trust (2003) links relevant topics to the National Curriculum:

Design and Technology: What happens next? Using other people's clothes KS3

English: Chaucer's 'The Pardoner's Tale' and the nature of pilgrimage KS3; *The Merchant of Venice* in Context (or other books and perspectives – see Edward Said) KS4; David Almond's *Skellig* and *Divine Messengers* KS3; Personal writing to celebrate cultural diversity KS4

History: How did Queen Elizabeth 1 and Emperor Akbar Keep control of their people? KS3

ICT: Rethinking Local Heroes KS4

Music: Exploring pulse, meter and rhythm in two mother-and child songs KS1; Exploring melodic structure, pulse and rhythm in music for dance KS2; Processes and Procedures: Comparing aspects of the blues and classical Indian approaches to improvisation KS3; Religious Education: Sacred writing and ancient scripts KS2; Creation and healers KS2

Visual and three-dimensional art: Identity KS4; Aboriginal art (could refer to ancient Indian Art and use of symbols) KS4.

Conclusion

People who demonstrate the dynamic response have the capacity to recreate, modify and synthesise a variety of influences in their environment and cultures. They often discreetly challenge the limitations of their communities, and independently select the elements of their identity they wish to preserve and those they wish to avoid or reject. Their independence of mind may have evolved through their experiences with their encounters with their communities and with wider society. However all the exemplifyers of the dynamic response see education as crucial to their development. It was often the most educated of my interviewees who articulated this response – S3 is a professional and P3 and P1 have university degrees.

7

Conclusion

'I think it's just going to go on blending, ending and evolving.'
(Quote by S3 in chapter six with reference to South Asian identity)

The representatives of South Asian communities featured in this study reveal a fascinating and complex world. They were constantly evaluating, deliberating and oscillating between two or more perspectives. They showed cultural and religious loyalty to their essential beliefs and values but also sought ways to interact with wider society, even in situations where there was tension. Contrasts and differences became creative as well as challenging.

The relationship between school and the communities can be improved in several ways. The dialectic between differences has potential for creativity. Asian cultures in the West can be seen as contributing an important reflexive element to UK culture and identities. 'Liberalism alone ... is an inadequate basis for multiculturalism' (Parekh quoted in Jaggi 2000: 6). Far from seeing the newer British cultures as having to be tolerated or assimilated, Parekh believes these cultures can provide valuable aids to understanding and evaluating one's own. As he says, 'If the dominant western culture has no interlocutor it lives in a hall of mirrors'. We need to acknowledge and exploit differences, not just overcome them. Organised and thoughtful engagement and discussions between the various communities is essential to reap the benefits of our culturally rich, vibrant environment. Evidence from the previous chapters suggests that there is much potential within the communities waiting to be tapped.

Diversity and disjuncture

The interviews elicited a range of responses. Some were shaped by the interviewee's experience and knowledge of another educational system and other cultural values and beliefs. But people responded differently in different situations or circumstances, or took different positions in the communities. Differing experiences and resources emanated from the different cultural beliefs and practices. Despite their varied cultures, historical and geographical backgrounds, those who had experienced a strict colonial education on the Sub-continent wanted their children to focus solely upon the core curriculum and academic subjects at school. Others expressed a more sophisticated understanding of the potential of education, especially the interviewees identified as radicals and those who adopted a dynamic response. These people critiqued the National Curriculum, expressed concern about the self-esteem and confidence of pupils, and recognised the value of self-expression through the Arts. Perspectives offered by the teachers and community representatives recognise the potential to address the differences and move from the ethnocentric and traditional approach to learning and education.

All pupils face a fundamental problem with the separation between the home and school and this is far more pronounced among those of South Asian origin. The South Asian social worker's diagram shown in chapter one is adapted in Figure 2.1 below to illustrate what the fieldwork described in this book discovered.

Figure 2.1: The social worker's diagram

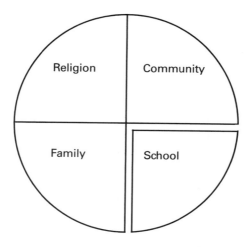

Schools seldom put the communities' beliefs and values on their agenda and teachers were under too much pressure to meet the government requirements to tackle cross-cultural issues. Nor were they given the training and resources they needed to do so. South Asian parents consistently expressed concern about the schools' ignorance of their beliefs and values. They remained cautious about engaging with the school and found PTAs disquieting rather than helpful.

Given the importance of cultural and religious identity for South Asian communities, it was unsurprising that the participants would all like to see more account taken of their beliefs and practices in the school and curriculum. A few criticised the ethnocentricism of the school ethos and curriculum and several spoke of the racism in society.

Incorporating cultural or religious dimensions into school life requires sensitivity. P1 thought teachers had become more aware of other cultures, including Islam, but spoke about the concerns within the communities about the interpretation of their religions:

P1:   I know in the primary school they have the religious education ... once in the year they may touch on Islam ... again that's their interpretation of it. Which is fine, I mean our children obviously have a bit more knowledge ... and in those times [past] people weren't so aware as they are now. Teachers ... make themselves more aware – find out more – talk to people to get a better view of it, so that they're not giving a view that may put down children in the class.

P1 indicates the importance of teachers not making interpretations of Islam that were biased or inaccurate. Collaboration with the communities could prevent this. This is one disjuncture of meaning and circumstance that requires urgent attention.

The issues raised in this book are not insurmountable. But unless they are carefully addressed, matters could become worse. A disjuncture between British society and South Asian communities could erupt in conflict when minority groups feel excluded and that their voices are unheard and unrepresented. Disjuncture between the National Curriculum and a teacher will make the teacher feel ignored and threatened by the overriding pressure to conform to ideas she does not always accept or cannot adapt but has to uphold. Such pressure may drive her to resign. And if there is a disjuncture between parents and teachers, negotiation is unlikely because the disjuncture is created by the build-up of misunderstandings of a social and cultural nature. However hard the teacher might try to include the communities' histories and beliefs in her lessons, she is constrained by the demands of the National Curriculum that she must answer to in terms of 'results'. However much parents may want to contribute to their children's education at school, they are constrained by their belief that the school represents the ideological stance of a secular British culture and takes no account of theirs.

This study revealed certain fundamental misunderstandings that inhibit progress. For example home/school meetings were found to be very one-sided. It is futile to invite South Asian parents to PTA meetings and parents' evenings, take no account of what they say, and then complain when they stop attending. The agenda for PTAs is not negotiated with the parents but imposed upon them, often ignoring what parents can accept or work with. And many schools refuse to understand why South Asian parents take their children out of school to visit the Subcontinent and study Islam, but think only of the inconvenience this causes. The reasons for such serious decisions should be conveyed to the staff and they should understand and respect them. The South Asian parents in this study wanted their children to do well at school but they also wanted them to experience positive identification with their South Asian communities and learn how to survive and mix in countries where other languages and beliefs than the school's prevail. Parents value such visits as an educational opportunity for their children but schools may fail to recognise their value.

To understand cultures and beliefs other than one's own, one has to empathise with a different point of view and be prepared for the fact that not all members of a community will hold identical views. And parents' views may alter according to the context of the encounter and the topic under discussion. How all the actors and contexts interact is complex and diverse.

Educational systems in the UK were seen to be quite different to those on the Subcontinent and this indicated another possible clash between reflective and pragmatic pedagogic ambitions, testing versus depth of understanding.

Parents and community representatives recognised that their children need more than education at school to live a successful life in the UK. They have to develop spiritual, social, communal abilities as well as intellectual. P1 tried to describe what 'success' might mean for a South Asian origin child:

P1:   To be a successful person – I think they've got to be confident. They've got to have this confidence which again doesn't come easily because when you're a child there's always issues going on in your head and around you ... obviously the education is obviously going to help – again the guidance whether it's at school or at home. Support from your family ... although I won't say that parents are always right ... I suppose you can look at success very differently ... Yes I'm just trying to think of a word in our own language that would um ... I can't think what it would be ... um ... something that would I mean the English wouldn't be one word – it would be – satisfying how – it would be like being satisfied with what you are doing – you know you find it rewarding – I think again it would be on both sides on the religious and the academic side. I think it could be something that is rewarding for you – and that you've kept your family happy as well because that comes in to it because not just an individual can – you know it's a family thing. You're doing something that they will be happy with and you will as well.

She concluded that the word 'fulfilled' would be better than 'successful'. P1 had difficulty with the word success and her interpretation certainly doesn't match Ofsted's definition. She aspired to integrate the collective within the individual, rather than to focus upon one single person achieving success. The dynamic responses articulated suggest a range of possibilities that still have to be exploited.

In chapter five, the representatives articulate the range of perspectives and flexibility that can engender cross-cultural communication. S3 recognised the way Sikhism aims to incorporate all religions, P1 registered the 'grey areas' of belief and religion that need to be explored and P2 emphasised the importance of broadmindedness. P3 thought that social and emotional development were implicit in her academic achievement. She noted that confidence was required to express a difference of opinion, and the support she has received from her family. Those who were most sceptical about their communities' potential insularity saw the school as a place where children could have greater social integration and understanding and were motivated to explore the cross-cultural experiences and knowledge they encountered. P3 in particular sees the social world of school as offering important social and cultural opportunities for the communities' children to discover. Similarly B3 and S3 welcome the multicultural character of the school. S3 and P3 drew upon their educational development and analytical abilities to transform and adapt their beliefs and practices and to critique the constraining and conservative elements in the communities, elements which teachers X and M both fear. Most importantly the children themselves were interested in comparing the differences between their homes and their school, displaying significant bicultural and multilingual skill.

It became increasingly clear that there were various avenues to pursue. If parents feel that their beliefs, values and experiences are validated in the school, the school may be more successful in engaging them and the community. And if parents clarify any meeting ground between the Mosque or Gurdwara and the school (Gregory: 1994), this could be built upon. The findings from my research were the catalyst for developing various consultations with the schools and communities that would involve parents and communities more closely in the life of the school, and ultimately improve the schools' educational provision for their children.

Working with the collaborative and collective elements in the communities

A central finding from the research was that members of South Asian communities tend to see themselves communally and operate that way. But confusions and misunderstanding can arise between collectivist communities and individualistic schools Rothstein-Fisch (1999), so schools would do well to invite parents to school in groups rather than individually. The benefits are two-fold. Parents would feel more confident and could support each other. Secondly, general cultural and religious or even political concerns could be aired and teachers would be addressing the needs of not just individual pupils but of whole groups of them.

The knowledge and enthusiasm I encountered when working with the communities made it possible to develop a range of initiatives to enhance communication between the local communities and schools. As a community co-ordinator and also a Race Equality Co-ordinator for schools, I was able to set up consultations, training days, conferences, workshops and ultimately local educational groups. Some of the initiatives informed by the discoveries outlined in this book are described below.

Having gained greater access to the communities during my research, I was able to work with educated young women and spokespeople in the communities to orchestrate a community consultation on education. This consultation was well attended by the young and the elderly of different religious and cultural backgrounds and confirmed their genuine concern about the educational welfare of South Asian children. We wrote a report and set out to develop an educational advisory group called *Kaamyaabi* an Urdu word which translates as 'to succeed'.

Kaamyaabi

Kaamyaabi synthesises the communal strength in the communities and the educational agendas of the schools. The group of representatives from the various South Asian communities, has had training on the National Curriculum and is in the process of working with schools to develop lesson plans that embed identity and cross-cultural exchanges into the curriculum. The organisation aims to draw upon the strengths of the communities, to increase the positive role models and to enhance the motivation and confidence of South Asian pupils to achieve highly at school. Three local schools are successfully piloting an exchange of knowledge with the communities and a university is evaluating the effects of this engagement. This has given us an opportunity to develop some of the ideas set out in other texts and guides for practitioners. For instance, *Here, There and Everywhere* (Richardson, 2005) and *Complementing Teachers* (Runnymede Trust, 2003) need to be part of a teacher's term plan for their lessons. The material is enhanced when trained and educated members of the communities work closely with the teachers to design and implement the sessions. Because this has administrative as well as organisational dimensions, it is essential for headteachers to give their full support. Designing systematic, clearly structured timetables with schools is essential to sustain the community link. Towards the end of this chapter there is an overview of sessions that were successfully designed and delivered collaboratively.

It is vital to understand the link between identity, self-esteem, motivation and attainment. Schools are unlikely to draw upon the initiatives suggested unless they can see a clear link between their need to raise attainment and to collaborate with the communities. Members of the Kaamyaabi group are also involved in supplementary support work, working closely with mainstream schools to increase the academic results for pupils in primary and secondary school (see Reay and Mirza, 2001) for insight into supplementary schools). At one secondary school, GCSE results were significantly improved when the school liaised with supplementary schools to prepare their pupils for exams. Mainstream teachers attended local community centres to provide extra classes to groups of Muslim pupils (see Cousins, 2005, 2006). This was combined with revision sessions and lessons led by community members outside the school context and these too have proved highly effective fostering the pupils' commitment to study. Attendance and involvement in the sessions has provided crucial evidence that South Asian role models, facilitators and educators strengthen pupils' beliefs in their ability to achieve.

Translations and interpretations

There is a pressing need for more interpreters in the school and also for more translations of school and National Curriculum documents so that parents can understand the school's focus and knowledge base better. Again this something community groups can assist with. But much time and skill is involved: schools will need to set a budget for translation and interpretation.

The interviewees expressed concern about feeling 'odd' and self-conscious at parents' evenings and this needs to be addressed. The disparities in the expectations of parental involvement and the importance of parents' contributions has still to be acknowledged by schools and communicated to the families, so they can feel valued and important. It is essential to empower parents and relatives so that genuine communication can take place.

Teacher training

How to avoid school practices that are directly or indirectly racist has to be made a compulsory part of all teachers training. The clique of white parents who prevented the South Asian parents from engaging more closely with the school, as described by teacher X, is a case in point. The concerns teacher M raised in relation to her lack of training around cross-cultural issues is worrying.

Reviewing pedagogic practices

The reasons for encouraging children to learn in a variety of ways may be difficult for parents to understand. Both the teachers and some community representatives identified the communities' general lack of appreciation for the Arts, or for child-centred learning and the importance of play. As many of the community members may have experienced only the colonial educational systems of the Subcontinent, teachers need to be able to explain the cognitive tools that are systematically being developed when children draw, build and translate their understanding through creative mediums such as music, art, poetry and technology. The emphasis on using initiative and working autonomously, as well as within groups, needs to be carefully considered and discussed with parents.

Organisational and curriculum adaptations

The recognition and respect for sacred spaces that South Asian parents mentioned indicates the need for prayer rooms. But the cultural and religious beliefs of the community need to be understood and integrated into the schools' curriculum. Understanding and connecting with current events and politics in Pakistan, Bangladesh and also the Punjab, as well as the history of the region, need to be part of the curriculum. Pupils and families should be encouraged to work on projects related to their beliefs and values for presentations at school.

All areas of the curriculum can be developed appropriately. In history for example, the effect of colonisation on developing countries and the different varied interpretations of history can be studied. South Asian pupils' 'lived experiences' of the Subcontinent could become part of geography. The skills of these bilingual pupils must be better acknowledged in language classes. The contributions early Islamic cultures made to science and mathematics should be taught to all pupils.

Suggested themes

- Broaden the curriculum to incorporate cultural diversity, for instance include the *suras* in poetry lessons. Collaboration between teachers and community representatives can greatly enrich the curriculum.

- Visits to the Subcontinent need to be acknowledged and used for the skills and knowledge they offer children. Education Bradford have published useful KS1 and KS2 works books for children to take abroad: *My journey to ...*, which provides educational focus for the children and parents who take it abroad.

- Valuing their experiences and drawing upon their experiences of contrasts will stimulate pupils' creativity and intellectual potential. Issues of identity, culture and race need to be discussed so that pupils are encouraged to draw upon their own experiences and knowledge. The aim is to ignite an ability to compare and contrast differences and to evaluate the strengths and weaknesses of different approaches to life.

The disjunctures between schools, the pupils and their communities are one form of institutional racism. It is important to recognise the racism children experience outside school as well and understand the impact on their self-esteem. Schools should reflect the population of the locality so that there are staff in a position of influence who share the knowledge base and background of the pupils.

Community development

The communities, too, can contribute to the education of their children by taking an active interest in what happens in school. They should invite teachers to visit the communities and actively challenge the schools to acknowledge the communities.

I hope that the research on which this book is based will demonstrate how to raise awareness. In the same way that I as the researcher needed to adapt and change my mindset during the fieldwork, the findings of this research may help to realise the need for more flexible thinking by educators. We need new pathways and opportunities that will allow reflection and exchange, drawing upon the resources of both the communities and the school. The research process is itself a catalyst for change. In particular the dialogic approach used in this study, asking questions and questioning our assumptions, could be applied to explore how teachers relate to communities, help them to evaluate their relationship with and attitudes to certain communities and encourage flexibility of approach and attitude. As Meyer (1991) observes, intercultural communication demands the skill to negotiate meanings as well as self-reflexive awareness.

As a researcher interacting with the communities, I would like to pay tribute to the participants' generous responses to my questions and the considerable insight they offered me. Although the transcripts convey some of the rich and varied views of the participants they can never convey the warmth, generosity and trust I was privileged to experience in these moments of exchange. The amalgam of neurological, psychological and cultural components of cross-cultural dialogues is not realisable in transcripts (Attinasi and Friedrich, 1996). Accordingly, I would like to encourage readers to venture out from their own domains of experience and discover this wealth for themselves, to question their own assumptions and draw upon their own imaginations to illuminate the data offered here by themselves

A model of curriculum development in a collaboration between *Kaamyaabi* and local schools

Food

Meanings attached to food in the Sikh Lunga.

The children were introduced to the significance of sharing and preparing food together and considered the concept of equality. Healthy eating was also integral to this topic.

Religion

The meaning of Ramadan: to understand what affects the body, life and feelings and the times for prayer and eating. Understanding the sense of communality and the experience of poverty. Understanding what Muslims gain from observing Ramadan. Food popular during Ramadan was tried and its nutritional value discussed.

Numeracy and Science

Understand the power of the zero and the Arabic design of patterns. Icebreaker – Punjabi numbers game. Looking at the scientific/astronomic buildings in Jaipur and the geometry of the Mosques. Children designed their own geometric patterns.

The elements

Understanding the symbolic meaning of water such as that Punjab is the name for water (five rivers flow into it); that there is a god of water; and the concept of purification attached in many religions to water; considering the Monsoon.

Poetry and literacy

Islamic poetry and scripts were compared with similar English poetry such as 'The Ancient Mariner' (simplified). After considering the 'Conference of Birds', the outer quest that became an inner quest, the children wrote their own story.

Art Landscapes

Looking at paradoxes: the gods of destruction and creation are illustrated throughout India. The children created their own picture of good and evil and discussed the difficulty categorising certain things simply as good or bad. This helped them discriminate between negative and positive elements in life.

RE: Debating God (s)

Looking at images of Gods from a variety of countries and religions: Considering: Is God Black or white? How helpful are images of God? Why is God seldom represented as a woman? Why there are no images of God in Islam.

Controversial cultural issues

Looking at the meaning of arranged marriages. Discussing mixed marriages. Considering the symbolic use of clothes as a form of protection: the use of veils in both East and West; the emotional attachment to customs and beliefs related to weddings.

engaging with communities, and teachers, to discover their diverse and fascinating worlds.

Finally, as this book aims to demonstrate the importance of developing ourselves as well as our insights, it offers a perspective on the ethnographic method. The data would not have yielded such rich knowledge if I had ignored the most challenging suggestion from the participants and community members: if I had not visited the Subcontinent. This degree of commitment to participation was key to any real awareness I was able to gain and would seem to be essential for those who aim to understand the greatest chasms in experience that certain representatives expressed. The visit made me profoundly aware of the importance of 'belonging', and of context that reaches across vast geographical boundaries into the hearts of those who continue to learn and share beliefs across continents within their own homes.

What follows is an outline of my methodology.

Addendum
Reflections on Methodology

I t is inevitable that the researcher will have what Fielding (1982: 96) calls 'muddy boots' or Marx calls 'grubby hands'. It would appear that participation observation, as Ditton (1977) suggests, is inherently unethical. Having clear procedures and practices that are written down and carried out overcomes some of this concern. So does metacognitive attentiveness – constantly being alert to ethical responsibilities as they arise, monitoring and appraising proceedings and being as clear and direct as possible to participants. I incorporated all these approaches to the best of my ability.

The privilege of being the researcher rather than a participant brought with it great responsibility. My position as researcher gave me considerable power, which was open to abuse. I was the one who selected whom to interview, decided whose story was most convincing or appropriate for my aims and objectives and what material to analyse and focus upon. Most importantly I was also the person people trusted with their perspectives and experiences, the one who would interpret and contexualise all they said. I was the one who made judgements and assessments about the validity of my participants' beliefs and practices. I was responsible for the orchestration of material for publication and circulation. Such a position demands careful attention to ethical issues and academic integrity. I had learnt from experience when working with Indigenous people of Australia that the researcher is someone of whom communities are justifiably wary. What do participants gain from the hours of openness and thoughtfulness they offer a researcher? Why should they offer anything at all, especially when past researchers have completely misunderstood cultural beliefs and reduced people to the position of 'natives' or 'subjects' to be observed. As Rosaldo (1986) observes: '[the] eye of ethnography [often connects with] the I of imperialism.' (p41).

In this study it is acknowledged that the researcher influences the interactions with the participants. She influences the data at two levels by actively selecting and orchestrating the situations and participants, and by interpreting the data. Burns (1977) suggests that all researchers unwittingly impose their own value judgements and that all observations are therefore theory laden. Thus it was essential to clarify my own experiences and perspectives prior to the research and, if necessary, during it.

A qualitative approach

A qualitative approach requires constant evaluations on the part of the researcher. It is essential to develop a process of critical inter-subjectivity, which encourages 'an open minded, responsive to evidence, accountable, critical-seeking manner' (Fay, 1996, p221) and also the development of understanding between the researcher and the participants. Differences between my background and the participants' meant that at first I had little understanding of their concerns and ways of life and had to adjust my own paradigms and beliefs dramatically to accommodate my findings. Fay points to the problems in research where imperialist apologists evaluated other cultures through the tinted glasses of their own society's values and beliefs and in the process re-established or reinforced a hierarchy of values and beliefs. To avoid reinforcing prejudice of this kind the researcher must maintain a self-critical and questioning attitude to her position and perspective. But this self-critical approach does not alone ensure accurate understanding of the participants' feelings, reflections and priorities. To achieve this one needs to take a carefully considered ethnographic approach.

The ethnographic approaches applied

An ethnographic approach allows for deeper exploration of such things as the social reality of a particular group and how their ideas are generated from a specific set of circumstances. It is thus sensitive to cultural variables and was considered highly appropriate to the focus of this study. This approach or method allows the researcher to explore another culture within the culture's own terms. As Athanases and Brice-Heath (1995) point out 'Learners are 'cultural' members for anthropologists who strive to understand how individuals be-come cultural carriers, transmitting and transforming ways of behaving, believing, and valuing within their social group.' (1995: 267). Interpreting the meaning of what has been said, however, is open to abuse and misinterpretation.

Critical and post-structuralist approaches aim to counter approaches used in the conventional ethnographic studies that reinforce a colonialist account of their participants' lives. Habermas (1973) challenged this hegemony and influenced the development of an *emancipatory model* (Kincheloe and McLaren, 1994) to address the concerns raised above and also to overcome intercultural misunderstanding. Identity politics (Hall: 1990) and anti-racist strategies, employed by Gillborn (1998) for example, also aim to address issues of stereotyping and prejudice. Post-structuralist approaches emphasise the dialogic process within ethnography and therefore the importance of 'writ[ing] the researcher into the text' (Gordan, Holland and Lahelm: 2002: 197). Keeping such concerns in mind, an ethnographic account needs to interrogate its own paradigms in relation to the perspectives in the wider society, to prevent endorsing versions of reality disseminated by those in power.

Interrogation is also important in order to justify the personal influence of the writer and researcher. Applying a symbolic interactionist approach to ethnography, Rock (2002) argues that ethnographic work is generally not orderly, often involving serendipity, creativity, hard work and good luck, all of which are likely to be subjective, not amenable to positivist evaluation. Rock argues that despite this limitation, it is valuable in terms of the light it can shed on the breadth and complexity of human relations. Its strength is in its depth of inquiry, flexibility and adaptability in the field. Rock sees the researcher as embedded in the process and subjectively engaged – part of the participant-led approach.

The participant/community-led approach

The participant/community-led approach involves flexibility and adaptability to the field. To maintain a sense of moral accountability the researcher must feel open to learn, discover and believe in her participants' experiences and accounts. I therefore designed my fieldwork in accordance with what the communities felt to be most significant. I sought to interrogate how I behaved and the decisions I made about the writers and researchers who have focused particularly upon these concerns. Participants played a significant role determining what and where to research the South Asian community members.

What to research

I had to adapt what to research in light of what I learnt from the participants. The whole process and focus was influenced by how people responded as well as what they discussed in interviews. I used a variety of instruments: interviews, observations and informal notes.

The key interviews amounted to 50, excluding the initial ones in the UK and on the Subcontinent. Adding in the interviews on the Subcontinent and those done when I was learning who was who, and what, how and when things happened brings the total to 79.

Interviews were initially based upon topics the Asian social workers and community representatives, and the gatekeepers who worked in the field, suggested, which would put the participants at ease. The participants wanted to answer philosophical questions such as 'What is it like to be a Pakistani?' or 'What does the word 'success' mean to you?' but needed more time to reflect. The participants sometimes asked to be asked such questions again later on in the interview. This was quite different from the abrupt or uncertain responses elicited when issues relating to school or the curriculum arose. So the participants' responses influenced the ultimate focus of the research.

The study had set out to identify the 'constructs of success' for teachers and communities. But it became apparent that success was a western concept predominant in educational jargon and literature; it turned out to be quite difficult for participants to define or discuss this concept in terms of their particular beliefs and practices. Topics relating to school were difficult to discuss as the parents interviewed generally knew little about what went on and were intimidated by questions around the school's curriculum and ideology. Their main knowledge and insights were regarding the learning they provided in their homes and in the communities. Their beliefs and values were key to understanding their constructs. One articulate community representative used the word 'fulfilment' to express her community's ideals, but still had to qualify this to signal that she used it in a group rather than individual sense. I learned that there were more important issues that summed up the whole situation between the school and community. I gradually became aware of the different territories that belonged exclusively to the school, South Asian communities in general or the different cultural and religious groups. This required a shift from an outsider's stance, which assumed a non-partisan approach, to a position where misconceptions about unequal partnership in the home/school relationship were challenged, recognising the problems and re-evaluating the constitution and qualities of this home situation.

Where to research

My initial decision to focus on interviewing South Asian community members in the UK had to change. Wanting to understand a community on its own terms, I realised on reflection that there was another dimension to the research that I needed to investigate. There was a unanimous belief that I should visit 'our' relatives, theirs and mine, on the Subcontinent to gain credible insights. The knowledge and connection this visit gave me was inestimable. It transformed my own sense of identity while also offering a profound understanding of attachments, which endure across the world. Visiting the Subcontinent involved far more resources, including specific funding from INTACH (The Indian National Trust for Art and Cultural Heritage) and more time than I had anticipated but it was definitive to my approach.

Critical self awareness

Critical self awareness is crucial to the ethnographer's understanding of how she affects the process and what she experiences or selects as evidence, even why she focuses on a particular area of concern (see Yonge, 1998). Every researcher holds particular values and beliefs that exist within a context and this context can be examined for the structural constraints and opportunities it allows. The ideas and values the researcher uses exist not only in a context but also within a time – within her own experiential and historical dimensions. It is therefore essential for the researcher to declare who she is, her perspectives, what influences she has imbibed and details about when and where data was gathered: to be explicit about what she did and why.

To achieve this I also kept a diary of my reflections, encounters, engagements and general experiences. I filled ten A4 notebooks over the two-years of data collection. An excerpt of my reflections is given below. It was taken from diaries written while on the Subcontinent and demonstrates some of the dilemmas I faced. It was during the visit to the Subcontinent that I was able to really explore the situations in homes in depth, as I had the opportunity to live with the families. This was also the time when I was most powerfully affected by my position and contexts: when my bicultural skills developed.

An example of my self-reflection:

> At times when I reflected upon my integrity as person, with certain thoughts and responses towards events, I felt unsure of whom I was in this particular context. My position as a researcher placed me close to being a voyeur and also to someone who didn't tend to come out in the open about what she felt and thought. I was uncertain about my own responses to things because I felt I had such limited experience to draw upon. My behaviour was in general passive, apart from my decisions to see people at certain times, and I questioned whether I had just adopted an 'acceptable female' demeanour. I seemed to hide myself and by contrast aimed to draw people out. I tried to be non-judgmental but often found myself reacting emotionally to situations and not necessarily expressing my feelings. I decided to monitor my judgmental responses by balancing them out with an alternative thought. For instance, I would see the dirt and chaos in the streets that appeared to be acceptable to others and feel uncomfortable but to compensate for this I would then register the ordered, austere, clean and aesthetically pleasing white marble Golden Temple. I would see the inequality on the streets and think about the support that family members could often assume to receive from each other ... As a researcher and yet having family ties in India, I found myself both an outsider and insider. My own identity seemed to be paradoxical at times. The closer I felt to the families I lived with, including my own, the more aware I became of the difference between my identity, behaviour and circumstances in the UK and in the Subcontinent, and yet I couldn't deny the importance of either. It would be interesting to consider Stuart Hall's constructs of identity in which he describes identity as something that is multifaceted and changeable in relation to context and time.

This excerpt illustrates the dilemmas I experienced with my own identity as a researcher and how this directed me to literature on identity that I had not looked at before. My disquiet about how to interpret the dirt and chaos in the streets continued to haunt me. After some reflection I realised I had greatly underestimated the economic costs of developing infrastructures needed for waste disposal or for the labour and technology third world countries can seldom afford. Codes of practice and expression of identity have to be understood in the context of socio-economic constraints. As well as the more theoretical and metaphysical awareness of identity, I became aware of the physical dimensions of identity relating to appearance and codes of practice. I had to question the foundations

of my own attitudes, values and beliefs and reappraise my interpretation of what I saw and experienced. I had continually to read
and upgrade my understanding of the participants. All this was
necessary to ensure that I did not enforce stereotypical views of the
community lives.

To counter any preconceptions about or stereotyping of South Asian
cultures in my selection and synthesis of data it was essential to
reveal my own predispositions and experiences (see Gillborn, 1998;
Mirza, 1998; Rakhit, 1998 and Thomas, 1995). These reflections are
captured on the next pages. Some of the problems I had to resolve
are outlined below. I embarked on this venture with more deficits
than assets.

The deficits were

- no knowledge of Asian cultural heritage
- no knowledge of any South Asian language
- no knowledge of living in a South Asian community
- no known contact with my South Asian roots
- no South Asian friends
- no South Asian religious experience

The assets were

- experience of interviewing Asian Muslim 6th form girls in a
  school
- researching the cultural values and beliefs of the Australian
  Indigenous people
- visiting India twenty years earlier
- a strong desire to understand South Asian communities and
  cultures
- the desire to confront issues of prejudice and ignorance towards minority groups, particularly Muslims in the UK

Comments from respondents sometimes prompted me to reflect
deeply. For example early on in the research process an elderly
representative of a local community told me that, politically speaking, as a Black woman, I was potentially among many under-
privileged, prejudiced people in society. She said that if I as the
researcher failed to recognise this, I was dismissing the realities experienced by more, rather than fewer, women of my colour living in
the UK. This forced me to reflect upon the context in which I was
working as well as the ways in which self-identity, circumstance and

perspective interact. It was also important for me to recognise that, my Asian appearance and middle class diction might well affect matters. To overcome this I had to spend some time establishing rapport with the participants, developing sensitivity to their issues and learning to respect their possible differences.

Gillborn (1998) warns against the potential for qualitative research to enforce stereotypes if it does not signal the power differential between the participants in certain contexts, for instance, where teachers and pupils are invited to discuss matters. The researcher, like the teacher, is a middle class academic with access to resources which are powerful and generally unlike the resources available to the participants. One way for the researcher to tackle this problem is to recognise that although she has certain advantages she is by no means as knowledgeable as her participants on certain matters. As Gillborn (1998) observes: 'participants in 'subordinate' positions (for they [can] lack formal training and institutional influence) sometimes understand more than their 'superiors'' (p52). The power imbalance is not to be ignored.

Stierer (1983) introduces the concept of a *black market* of information – unrecorded, intuitive thinking that is part of the way of making sense of phenomenological data. So I needed to be conscious and revealing about unofficial data such as my reflections, and to be upfront about these influences during the research process. Notably Thomas (1995), writing about teachers' perspectives, points out that 'An autobiography will add to reliable knowledge if it makes use of individual experience' (p99). Rakhit (1998), who writes as both a teacher and an Indian living in the UK, describes how her experience and predisposition has influenced her interpretation of the material she collected for her PhD research.

Participatory involvement

The ethnographic approach I used is identified as participatory involvement. Participatory involvement raises problems in terms of the degree of detachment and participation and the extent to which the researcher can remain detached and objective. Sarsby (1980), who studied economically deprived families, notes that the ethnographer will always be oscillating between empathy and repulsion, home and strangeness, and seeing and not seeing. To act with a clear conscience the researcher must be aware of: her level of detachment and involvement, her emotional reaction to different participants and her own prejudices and limitations.

The researcher's story

The following extract from my diary helps reveal how my background might have influenced my position and perspectives as the researcher when I visited South Asia and researched in the South Asian community.

I am of South Asian origin. Most of my early life was spent in a rural community in the UK. As one of a family of four children, with a mother who was divorced and taught English at a local public school, our family was 'different'. Furthermore, my maternal grandmother was Austrian-Italian and my mother, though half Asian, had been born in Venice and educated at a progressive co-educational boarding school in the UK; being 'Indian' was obscure and inaccessible. It had its moments of recognition when we were told to 'go black home' or told that the Pakistanis who lived next to our classmates' relatives in London 'pissed in the garden'. It also had moments of frustration for our more 'interested' friends who expected us to have an exotic language or knowledge we didn't have. There were numerous ways in which the business of being Black or Asian was an anachronism, certainly an anomaly. I felt drawn to identify with the Elizabethan age as the historical novels created such a sense of romance around that era. I wanted to have white hands and cringed at the thought of being the little page who stood in the corner and fanned the courtier, who came from a more 'primitive' world. Over time I felt I knew how to behave only in England, whatever I felt about it. By my twenties I still hadn't tried to get in touch with any South Asian people. My own brief impression of an Asian doctor's surgery in East Ham in London was that it was conservative and insular, and I realise now I had a prejudiced view of South Asian communities. I certainly did not identify with them.

However, when I chose to visit India in my early twenties I was suddenly aware that I could slip into the crowds and disappear, yet belong in a way I had never felt I could in the UK. Although, I didn't find any roots something stirred within me.

Twenty years later when I set out to explore the perspectives of minority communities and their relationship with schools, it was the South Asian people rather than any other minority group who welcomed me into their homes and community centres. They always asked me where I came from and assumed I was one of them and so I decided to take another plunge and find out who we are. I decided that these people were related to me and that beyond our differences we had some connection.

To start with, the researcher arrives in the field as an outsider. This gives her a perspective that is quite different to what it will become. This initial position is liminal, on the margins, and this has certain advantages. Perception is likely to be a sharpest due to being on the border or coming from outside and not yet immersed. There is though a paradox here in that it is only by closer involvement with the groups and their cultures that subtleties are realised and the real issues come to light. So it is invaluable to be able to assume both an insider's and an outsider's position.

The participatory involvement applied in this study and my inter-action with my respondents fits with Byram's (1998) matrix of four different intercultural competences (see chapter two). I needed to demonstrate intercultural competence in my interactions with another 'culture'. Byram's four processes can be applied to the processes by which I as ethnographic researcher sought to challenge my own ethnocentric attitudes.

First, *savoir faire* [knowing what to do] requires openness towards another culture and the ability to see one's own for its weaknesses as well as its strengths, to distance oneself from it. This could be seen as equivalent to the initial stage the researcher must engage in on entering a field: being accepted into another cultural group when the members recognise these qualities and this openness.

Second, *savoir apprendre* [knowing what to learn] involves collecting data and analysing it, and requires the ability to decentre and see situations within their context. This was a central reason for my visit to the Subcontinent, a development from the initial methodology.

Third, *savoir* [knowledge] to understand the new culture in terms of the meanings it holds for the cultural group: how their particular values and beliefs are applied to their particular contexts and situations. The key factors particular to the culture became apparent to me once I understood the relevant cultures in the Subcontinent as well as in England.

Fourth and finally, to apply all *savoirs* to real situations, for example using my experiences on the Subcontinent to develop my under-standing of the situation for South Asians living in the UK.

However, participatory involvement can deceive both the researcher and especially the participants. Problems of duplicity inherent in the researcher's self-identity have to be addressed. As a visitor to the field rather than an inhabitant, the researcher is placed in a pre-carious position in terms of her participation. I wished to create a sense of belonging or acceptance within the group I was studying. This meant that when I left the field I might betray the trust that will have developed because the participants allowed me to belong. My loyalty is not the same as for those who live permanently in the field. So there is a danger that duplicity can exist, though attachment to the field can also develop. Abu-Lughod (1986), researching the Bedouin community anticipates her loss and sadness after leaving the field: 'It is the quiet life I will miss. There is no loneliness, always someone to sit with. I feel so much part of something here. I don't remember ever feeling that before' (pxiii). In my case, I never withdrew from involvement with the communities either personally and professionally.

This reflection indicates how a shared and consciously self-critical approach can develop between researcher and participants. However, these adaptations cannot replace a clear set of ethical standards and codes.

Ethics

To achieve a degree of immersion, however limited, into the lives of others, an ethnographic approach can intrude on the subjects' privacy. And because it often entails an exploration of a disempowered or culturally divergent group, the researcher can expose the participants to further misunderstanding and reinforce stereotypical views about them. This can have serious ethical repercussions in a political, social and emotional sense. Stanfield (1994) writes of conduct in qualitative research 'as a structured power relationship and as an intricate process of creating, interpreting, and disseminating knowledge' (p179). So there are fundamental ethical considerations and also subtle and complex issues that underlie close, often emotional encounters that require sensitive practice.

Participants' right to privacy, confidentiality and anonymity

The researcher must ensure that all participants are aware of their rights. This is particularly important in a study that concerns another culture, and where the participants may not be aware of all their rights, or may feel dominated by the researcher or the gatekeepers. To try to address these concerns I gave the participants in my study a clear code of ethics to agree to, which set out their rights when they read the transcripts to withdraw themselves or any comments they felt could be misinterpreted. They were encouraged to comment on the overall understanding I gained and thus how I con-texualised their comments.

The participant observer/participatory approach, the emancipatory model and the data driven approach that I adopted all drive the data collection method and analytical process. As Miles and Huberman (1994) argue, the strength of the qualitative, grounded approach is that it has a:

> strong handle on what 'real life' is like ... the influences of the local context are not stripped away but taken into account ... [and that this emphasis on people's lived experience] is well suited for locating meanings people place on the events, processes, and structures in their lives: their 'perceptions, assumptions, prejudgements, presup-positions' (van Manen, 1977) and for connecting these meanings to the *social world* around them'. (p10, emphasis in the original).

This overall approach complements the ethical, social and political issues that arose during the literature review, in particular the need to raise the voices of the marginalised and under-represented in the home/school relationship and understand them better from their own perspectives. Such a combined approach also addresses the concerns that Argyle (1992) and Waldrop (1992) raise about internal validity, generalisations and various reductionist approaches failing to achieve ecological validity.

Moving into the communities

My adaptations to the research design to accommodate what the participants and community representatives prioritised showed them that I took their perspectives seriously and was eager to learn. My understanding depended on gaining access to the communities: the range of perspectives and positions I discovered were founded upon this access. I relied on certain community representatives or gatekeepers when I first tried to access the communities and I learned that the people the gatekeepers give the researcher access to also restrict her. As Klein (1976) observed: 'Social science is not en-gaged by 'industry' or organisations but by individuals in gate-keeping or sponsorship or client roles. The outcome, therefore, is always mediated through the needs and resources, and roles of such individuals' (p225).

It was vital to established good relationships with the various com-munity leaders and their contacts as relationships within the com-munities were closely interwoven. Furthermore, I discovered, there was a general lack of trust towards the schools within the communities, which severely limited its capacity to identify respondents for me to work with. This was because many of the South Asian parents at the school did not use it as a community link and kept relatively distant from it, merely taking their children to and from the school gates. This crucial factor influenced a major change in the research design.

As well as problems of access there were problems of language, which I discovered in the first term I was at the school. In an initial round of interviews with parents from the main school it was discovered that some parents were unable to speak English sufficiently and therefore their children had to translate. This meant that understandings and insights were limited, especially when taken from transcripts.

I became aware that my initial approach could be identified as an outsider's methodology, being school-based. As I gained greater insight into the communities' contexts, I realised that a community-based rather than school-based approach would be helpful. One way to pre-empt making too rapid a cause/effect judgement before there is clear connection between the two, is to check out 'rival explanations, ruling out spurious relations, or using extreme cases' (Miles and Huberman, 1994:258). This change also heralded a dramatic change in my awareness of the school/home relationship. The criteria for selecting certain participants was no longer in terms of their relationship with the main school but rather whether the representatives reflected the range of perspectives in the communities.

In the search for appropriate representation I reconsidered people I had met in the first year of fieldwork and, in the light of what I learned about the communities, I identified specific individuals to interview in greater depth. Here there was a degree of purposive sampling since those chosen as the final representatives were those best able to represent the views of the communities. The choice was influenced by those encountered in the initial supportive round of interviews, both in terms of advice given as to who would be a good spokesperson and also in terms of who was actually encountered. Interview selection can be affected by the fact that people may select themselves and also others (see Walsh, 1998) and I needed to get beyond this limitation. I needed people who:

- were articulate in English language
- who showed some understanding of the objectives of the research

- had the capacity to reflect on and develop their ideas
- were confident and had a sense of responsibility about their community
- had rapport with the researcher
- had a warm and welcoming approach
- who belonged to the community even if they did have reservations about it, and who nonetheless identified with its South Asian elements
- were not too dominating about their own agendas and unable to answer questions
- were interested in the project
- were not hostile to their communities

For various reasons the number of participants to access was limited. Many potential participants were too busy with work and children to care for so could not give of their time. Others were not fluent enough in English to be able to answer some of the in-depth questions I needed to ask. Still others were shy and not confident enough to be part of the research. Finally, my own bias for including only those enthusiastic about their involvement in the research ruled out some people, as I wanted to discuss issues as extensively as possible. This was admittedly a limitation as I might have been able to access more people if I had had longer to build up rapport over more than one year. Therefore to some degree I used convenience sampling in terms of availability.

The choice of respondents to augment the initial group of parents was thus dependent on several factors. I visited various community centres, social workers and community representatives as well as the schools. I did not access all the people who became interviewees right away. Although certain participants were insightful and articulate, they were unsuitable as key representatives if I was to ensure a balance of perspectives from each cultural group.

The key participants were recommended by members in the communities for their knowledge of cultural and religious values and beliefs. They were chosen because they could discuss South Asian practices and beliefs, and because they were bilingual. The fieldwork with the families had revealed that the parents were not necessarily those most able to discuss or comprehend issues related to their children's schooling. The assumption made in the educational system that pupils live in separate, independently orientated nuclear families was evident in only only one instance. The pupils as well as the parents saw themselves as members of *communities* and not just families. Pupils often relied upon aunts, uncles, grand-parents, older siblings and community members who were not related through blood to help them in various ways, including with their schoolwork. Thus it was entirely appropriate to interview members of the communities in order to understand the views of parents. Often older siblings, aunts, grandparents (if more educated than the parents) and other relatives were more aware of these issues. Thus one twenty-two year old sibling, unmarried and living with her family, who was very articulate about the influences of her own education, her younger siblings' and her parents' experiences, became an interviewee in the last phase of the fieldwork.

It was possible for me, as a researcher and not a teacher working full time in a classroom, to access the communities because I had time to consider various avenues to pursue. Below are some suggestions for approaching communities derived from my experience.

Guidelines for teachers approaching communities

- Set aside 3-6 months to work on it: you need patience, per-severance and bicultural competence

- Caution: potential key protagonists – South Asian people already linked to schools – may feel disheartened or cynical about collaborating with school. Because of the lack of structural development in schools to create a platform for sustainability, initiatives may flounder and fail

- Visit community centres and identify gatekeepers

- Take note of the varied perspectives in this book that are represented by different responses and initially focus on contacting people who are suitable spokespeople and easily accessible. Approaching a parent who prefers to avoid con-tact may by difficult

- Developing relationships with just two or three individuals is a good start

- Engage in one or two social and cultural activities; enjoy them and build rapport with people

- Build a reputation and identity based upon your reliability, consideration, openness

- Do not promise things you cannot deliver

- Ask for the communities' perspectives – do not focus on school agendas before understanding the communities' priorities

- Do some exploring and re-evaluation of your own beliefs and practices

I have tried to convey the brilliance of the field by drawing predominately upon what my participants said. However, this distilled version does not fulfil the criteria of engagement and collaboration. The previous chapters identified some options, but every context varies and provides opportunities for other initiatives ...

References

Abu-Lughod, L (1986) *Veiled Sentiments*. Berkeley. University of California Press.

Ackah, W (2006) Aiming where precisely ? An assessment of short-term urban educational initiatives on Black communities in Britain. *Local Economy*.

Alldred, P, David, M, Edwards, R (2001) Minding the Gap: Children and Young People Negotiating Relations between Home and School. In: *Children, Home and School: Regulation, Autonomy or Connection?* Edited by R. Edwards, London. Routledge/Falmer.

Armstrong, K (2000) *The Battle for God. Fundamentalism in Judaism, Christianity and Islam*. London, Harper Collins.

Argyle, M (1992) *The Social Psychology of Everyday Life*. London, Routledge.

Athanases, S, T and Brice-Heath, S (1995) Ethnography in the Study of the Teaching and Learning of English. *Research in the Teaching of English*, 29: 3. pp. 263-287.

Attanasi, J and Friedrich, P (1996) Dialogic Breakthrough: Catalysis and Synthesis in Life-Changing Dialogue. In: *The Dialogic Emergence of Culture*. Edited by Dennis Tedlock and Bruce Mannheim. Chicago, University of Illinois Press.

Ballard, R (1994) Introduction: The Emergence of Desh Pardesh. In: *Desh Pardesh: The South Asian Presence in Britain* (1994). Edited by R. Ballard. London, Hurst and Co.

Ballard, R (1994) Differentiation and Disjunction among the Sikhs. In: *Desh Pardesh: The South Asian Presence in Britain*. (1994). Edited by R. Ballard. London, Hurst and Co.

Barwuah, A (1998) Background Noise. *Guardian Education*. 13/ 04/98.

Basit, T (1997) I Want More Freedom But Not Too Much: British Muslim Girls and the Dynamism of Family Values. *Gender and Education*. 09: 04 pp. 425-439.

Batsleer, J; Chantler, K and Burman, E (2003) Responses of Health and Social Care Staff to South Asian Women who Attempt Suicide and/or Self-Harm. *British Journal of Social Work Practice*.

Baudrillard, J (1988) *America*. London, Verso.

Beck, U (1991) *Risk Society: Towards a New Modernity*. (Translated by M. Ritter) London, Sage.

Bhatti, G (1999) *Asian children at home and at school*. London, Routledge.

Bhimji, Z (1990) Live for the Sharam and die for Izzat. In: *Identity, Community Culture, Difference*. London, Lawrence and Wishart.

Billig, M (1987) *Arguing and Thinking: a Rhetorical Approach to Social Psychology*. Cambridge, Cambridge University Press.

Blackledge, A (1998) The Institutionalisation of Inequality: the Initial Teacher Training National Curriculum for Primary English as Cultural Hegemony. *Educational Review*. 50:01 pp.55-65.

Blackledge, A (2000) Power Relations and the Social Construction of 'Literacy' and 'Illiteracy'. Experiences of Bangladeshi Women in Birmingham. In: *Reading and writing different worlds*. Edited by John Benjamins. Multilingual Literacies. Amsterdam.

Bourdieu, P (1992) *Language and Symbolic Power*. Cambridge, Polity Press.

Bourdieu, P and Passeron. (1977) *Reproduction in the Society, Education and Culture*. Los Angeles, Sage.

Bourdieu, P and Passeron, J.C (1979) *The Inheritors: French students and their relation to culture*. Translated by R Nice. Chicago, University of Chicago Press.

Bowkett, S (1997) *'Imagine That ... ': A Handbook for Creative learning Activities in the Classroom*. Edited by Carol Thompson and Chris Griffin, Network Educational Press.

Burns, T (1977) The BBC. London: Macmillan. In: *Handbook of Qualitative Research*. Edited by N. Denzin and Y. Lincoln (1994). London, Sage.

Byram, M (1998). Cultural Identities in Multilingual Classrooms. In: *Beyond Bilingualism*. Edited by J. Cenoz and F. Genesee. Clevedon, Multilingual Matters.

Castells, M (1997) *The Power of Identity*. Oxford, Malden, Blackwell.

Chatterjee, P (1997) *The Present History of West Bengal: Essays in Political Criticism*. Delhi, Oxford University Press.

Clark, K and Clarke, M. P (1947) 'Racial Identification and Preference in the Negro Children'. In: *Readings in Social Psychology*. Edited by T. M. Newcombe and E.L. Hartley. New York, Holt.

Coles, M and Chilvers, P (2003) *Education and Islam: developing a culturally inclusive curriculum*. School Development Support Agency, Leicester City Council. Email: Maurice.coles@dsdsa.net.

Commission for Racial Equality (2000) *Learning for All; Standards for Racial Equality in Schools*. Commission for Racial Equality.

Conway, G (1997). *Islamaphobia, its features and dangers:* A consultation paper issued by the Runnymede Commission on British Muslims and Islamaphobia. London, Runnymede Trust.

Conway, M and Haque, S (1999). Overshadowing the Reminiscence Bump: memories of a struggle for independence. *Journal of Adult Development:* 06:01.pp. 35-44.

Cousins, L (2005) *Achievement and Incentives Scheme Project evaluation*. Liz Cousins Ltd.

Dadzie, S (2000) *Toolkit for Tackling Racism in Schools*. Stoke on Trent, Trentham

De Rijike V and Sinker, R (1996) 'Rubbish Reading, Visual Arts and Media in the National Curriculum. In: *Interpreting the New National Curriculum*. Edited by Andrews, R. Middlesex, Middlesex University Press.

Dickinson, S (1997) Towards a Developmental Framework: empowering youth-work with young Asian women. In: *Race and Groupwork*. Edited by T. Mistry and A. Brown. London, Whiting and Birch.

Ditton, J (1977) *Part-time Crime*. London, Macmillan.

Donaldson, M (1978) *Children's Minds*, London, Fontana.

Edwards, C. P (1995) Parenting Toddlers. In: *Handbook of Parenting*. Edited by MH Bornstein. Hillsdale, Erlbaum.

Fanon, F (1990) *The Wretched of the Earth*. (Reprinted) London, Penguin Books.

Fay, B (1996) Can We Understand Others Objectively? In: *Contemporary Philosophy of Social Science*. Oxford, Blackwell.

Fielding, N (1982) Observational Research on The National Front. In: *Social Research ethics*. Edited by M. Bulmer. London, Macmillan.

Gardner, K and Shukar, A (1994) 'I'm Bengali, I'm Asian, and I'm Living Here': The changing identity of British Bengalis. In: Desh Pardesh: *The South Asian Presence in Britain*. (1994). Edited by R. Ballard. London, Hurst and Company.

Ghouri, N (1998) 'Colour-Blind' Teacher Training Condemned. *Times Educational Supplement*. 17/7/98.

Ghouri, N (1999) Section 11 staff face redundancy. *Times Educational Supplement*. 15/01/ 99.

Ghuman, P (1999) *Asian Adolescents in the West*. Leicester: British Psychological Society.

Giddens, A (1994) Living in a Post-Traditional Society. In: *Reflective Modernization*. U; Beck, Giddens, A and Lasch, S. Oxford, Polity Press.

Gillborn, D (1998) Racism and the Politics of Qualitative Research: learning from Controversy and critique. In: *Researching Racism in Education*. Edited by P. Connolly and B. Troyna. Buckingham, Open University Press.

Gillborn, D and Gipps, C (1996) *Recent Research on the Achievements of Ethnic Minority pupils*. London, Ofsted.

Gillborn, D and Youdell, D (2000) *Rationing Education: Policy, practices, reform and equity*. Buckingham, Open University Press.

Ginnis, P (2002) *'The Teachers' Toolkit': Raise Classroom Achievement with Strategies for Every Learner*. Wales, Crown House Publishing Ltd.

Gool, S (1998) Voices Still to be Heard. Unpublished Thesis. Queensland University of Technology, Australia.

Gordan, T, Holland, J and Lahelma, E (2002) Ethnographic Research in Educational Settings. In: *Handbook of Ethnography*. Edited by P. Atkinson, A. Coffey, S. Delamont, J. Lofland and L. Lofland. London, Thousand Oaks. New Delhi, Sage.

Gregory, E (1994) 'Cultural Assumptions and Early Years' Pedagogy: The Effect of the Home Culture on Minority Children's Interpretation of Reading in School.' *Language, Culture and Curriculum*. 7: 2 pp.111-124.

Habermas, J (1973) *Theory and Practice*. Boston, Beacon Press (First published in German, 1963).

Hall, S (1990) Cultural Identity and Diaspora. In: *Identity: Community Culture, Difference*. Edited by J. Rutherford. London, Lawrence and Wishart.

Hamers, H and Blanc, M (1989) *Bilinguality and Bilingualism*. Cambridge, Cambridge University Press.

Harber, C (2004) *What's the Damage? Schooling as violence: how schools harm pupils and societies.* London, RoutledgeFalmer.

Hardy, J and Vieler-Porter, C (1988) Race, Schooling and the Educational Reform Act. In: *Structures and Strategies. Racism and Education.* Edited by D. Gill, B. Mayor and M. Blair. Open University Press and Sage.

Holt, J (1996) Learning to be 'Stupid'? In: *Readings for Reflective Teaching in the Primary School.* Edited by A. Pollard. London, Continuum.

Hutnik, N (1991) *Ethnic Minority Identity: a social psychological perspective.* Oxford, Clarendon Press.

Inhelder, B and Piaget, J (1958) *The Growth of Logical Thinking from Childhood to Adolescence.* London, Routledge and Kegan Paul.

Jaggi, M (2000) First Among the Equalisers. *The Guardian Profile.* Bhikhu Parekh 21/10/00. (Ref: The Parekh report, (2000) London, Profile Books.

Jones, C, Maguire, M and Watson, B (1996) First Impressions: Issues of Race in School-Based Teacher Education. *Multicultural Teaching* 15:1. pp.34-43.

Jones, C, Maguire, M and Watson, B (1997) The School Experience of some Minority Ethnic Students in London Schools during Initial Teacher Training. *Journal of Education for Teaching,* 23: 2.pp.131-145.

Jordan, J (1997) Cited in: *Culture, Economy, Society.* Edited by A.H. Halsey, H. Lauder, P. Brown and A. S. Wells. Oxford, Oxford University Press.

Kakar, S (1996) *The Colors of Violence.* Chicago. London, University of Chicago Press.

Karran, S (1997) 'Auntie-ji, please come and join us, just for an hour.' The role of bilingual education assistant in working with parents with little confidence. In: *Home-School in Multicultural Settings.* Edited by J. Bastiani. London, David Fulton.

Kearney, C (1996) By No Means Marginal: bicultural perspectives in the new National Curriculum. In: *Interpreting the New National Curriculum.* Edited by Richard Andrews. Middlesex, Middlesex University Press.

Khan, N (1992) Asian Women's Dress From Burqah to Bloggs: changing clothes for changing times. In: *Chic Thrills.* Edited by J. Ash and E.Wilson. London, Harper Collins.

Kincheloe, J. L and McLaren, P.L (1994) 'Rethinking Critical Theory and Qualitative Research'. In: *Handbook of Qualitative Research.* Edited by N. K. Lincoln and Y.S. Lincoln. London, Sage.

Klein, R (2000) Uniquely Sikh. *Times Educational Supplement* 28/04/00.

Lakoff, G (1987) *Women, Fire and Dangerous Things: What Categories Reveal about the Mind.* Chicago: Chicago, University Press.

Lee, H (1963) *To Kill a Mocking Bird.* London, Penguin.

Levy, R (1995) Essential Contrasts: differences in parental ideas about learners and teaching in Tahiti and Nepal. In: *Parental Belief Systems their origins, expressions and consequences.* Edited by S. Harkness and C. M. Super. New York, Guilford.

Lewis, P (1994) Being Muslim and Being British: The dynamics of Islamic reconstruction in Bradford. In: *Desh Pardesh: The South Asian Presence in Britain.* Edited by R. Ballard. London, Hurst and Company.

Luthra, M (1997) *Britain's Black Population.* Aldershot, Arena.

Meyer, M (1991) Mediating Languages and Cultures: In: *Towards an intercultural theory of foreign language education.* Edited by D. Buttjes and M. Byram. Clevedon, Multilingual Matters.

Miles, M and Huberman, M.B (1994) *Qualitative Data Analysis.* Second edition. London, Sage.

Millett, A (1998) Race to the Fore. *Times Educational Supplement,* 10/7/98.

Mirza, M (1998) 'Same Voices, Same Lives?': Revisiting Black Feminist Standpoint Epistemology. In: *Researching Racism in Education.* Edited by P. Connolly and B. Troyna. Buckingham, Open University Press.

Modood, T, Beishon, S and Virdee, S (1994) *Changing Ethnic Identities.* London, Policy Studies Institute.

Modood, T (1997) Culture and Ethnicity. In: Modood *et al,* eds. *Ethnic Minorities in Britain: Diversity and Disadvantage.* London, Policy Studies Institute.

Mohanty, C, T (1997) On Race and Voice: Challenges for liberal education in the 1990s. In: *Culture, Economy, Society.* Edited by A.H. Halsey, H. Lauder, P. Brown and A.S. Wells. Oxford, Oxford University Press.

Morgan, C, L and Joy, G.T (1999) Intercultural Understanding between the Researcher and Researched. AILA 1999 Tokyo, Conference proceedings, JACET: Tokyo CD Rom.

Morgan, S (1995) *My place.* London, Virago Press.

My Journey to ... (2004) Key stage 1 and 2. Education Bradford, Bradford Trading Central Team. Bradford BD4 7EB.

Newham Asian Women's project and Newhan Innercity Multifund (1998) *Growing Up Young, Asian and Female in Britain: A report on self-harm and suicide.* London Borough of Newham.

Nicholls, G (1999) *Learning to Teach. A handbook for primary and secondary school teachers.* London, Kogan Page.

Ofsted (2001) *Managing Support for the Attainment of Pupils from Minority Ethnic Groups.* October 2001. Ref HMI 326.

Parker-Jenkins, M (1995) *Children of Islam: A teacher's guide to meeting the needs of Muslim pupils.* Stoke-on-Trent, Trentham Books.

Patel, G (1997) Communities in Struggle: Bengali and Refugee Groupwork in London. In: *Race and Groupwork.* Edited by T. Mistry and A. Brown. London, Whiting and Birch.

Paulston, C. B (1992) Sociolinguistic Perspectives in Bilingual Education. In: *Biculturalism: some reflections and speculations.* Edited by C. B. Paulston. Clevedon, Multilingual Matters.

Phinney, S. J (1989) Stages of Ethnic Identity Development in Minority Group Adolescents. *Journal of Early Adolescents,* 9. pp. 34-49.

Piaget, J (1973) *The Psychology of Intelligence,* New Jersey, Adam and Co (first published by Routledge and Kegan Paul 1950).

Piaget, J (1980) *Adaptation and Intelligence,* Chicago, University of Chicago Press.

Qureshi, S and Khan, J (1989) *The Politics of Satanic Verses. Unmasking Western attitudes.* Leicester, Muslim Communities Studies Institute.

Rakhit, A (1998) Silenced Voices: Life history as an approach to the study of South Asian women teachers. In: *Researching Racism in Education: Politics, Theory and Practice*. Edited by P. Connolly and B. Troyna, Buckingham, Open University Press.

Rampton, B (1995) *Crossing Language and Ethnicity among Adolescents*. London, Longman.

Rassool, N (1999) Flexible Identities: Exploring Race and Gender Issues Among a Group of Immigrant Pupils in an Inner-City Comprehensive School. *British Journal of Sociology of Education*, 20: 01. pp.23-26.

Rattansi, A (1992) Changing the subject? Racism, culture and education. In: *'Race' Culture and Difference*. Edited by J. Donald and A. Rattansi. London, Open University and Sage.

Reay, D and Mirza, H.S (2001) Black Supplementary Schools: Spaces of Radical Blackness. In: *Educating Our Black Children*. Edited by R. Majors, London, RoutledgeFalmer.

Richardson, R (2005) *Here, There and Everywhere: belonging, identity and equality in schools*. Trentham Books in association with Derbyshire Education Department.

Rock, P (2002) Symbolic Interactionism and Ethnography. In: *Handbook of Ethnography*. Edited by P. Atkinson, A. Coffey, S. Delamont, J. Lofland and L. Lofland. London, Sage.

Rosaldo, R (1989) *Culture and Truth: the remaking of social analysis*. Boston, MA, Beacon Press.

Rothstein-Fisch, C, Greenfield, P.M and Trumbull, E (1999). Bridging cultures with classroom strategies. *Educational Leadership*. 56: 7 pp. 64-67.

Runnymede Trust (2003) *Complementing Teachers; A Practical Guide to Promoting Race Equality in Schools*, Granada Learning.

Rutherford, J (1990) A Place Called Home: Identity and the cultural politics of difference. In: *Identity, Community Culture, Difference*. Edited by J. Rutherford. London, Lawrence and Wishart.

Said, E.W (1993) *Culture and Imperialism*. London, Vintage.

Said, E.W (1997) *Covering Islam*. London, Vintage.

Sarsby, J, Coffield, F and Robinson, P (1980) *A Cycle of Deprivation? A case study of four families*. London, Social Science Research Council.

Schopen, F (2003) Educational grant for minorities under threat. *Community Renewal News* 14/03/03.

Searle, J (1995) *The Construction of Social Reality*. London, Penguin.

Shaw, A (1994) The Pakistani Community in Oxford. In: Desh Pardesh: *The South Asian Presence in Britain*.Edited by Roger Ballard. London, Hurst and Company.

Short, G and Carrington, B (1996) Anti-racist Education, Multiculturalism and the New Racism. *Educational Review* 48:01.pp. 65-77.

Smith, Z (2000) *White Teeth*. London, Hamish Hamilton

Spencer, C (2000) Caught in a Cultural Chasm. *Times Educational Supplement*. 02/06/00.

Stanfield, J. H (1994) Ethnic modeling in Qualitative Research. In: *Handbook of Qualitative Research*. Edited by N. Denzin and Y. Lincoln. London, Sage.

Sushma Rani Puri (1997) Working with parents in a Multicultural Secondary School. In: *Home-School in Multicultural Settings*. Edited by J. Bastiani. London, David Fulton.

Tawney, R. H (1964) *Equality* (first published 1931), Liverpool, Allen and Unwin.

Tedlock, D and Mannheim, B (Eds) (1995) *The Dialogic Emergence of Culture*. Chicago, University of Ilinois.

Thomas, D (1995) *Teachers' Stories*. Buckingham, Open University Press.

Thompson, J (1992) *Editor's Introduction to: Language and Symbolic Power by Pierre Bourdieu*. Edited by John Thompson. Cambridge, Polity Press.

Tomlinson, Sally (1994) *Ethnic Minorities. Involved Partners or Problem Parents? In: Parental Choice and Education*. Edited by JM. Halstead. London, Kogan Page.

Troyna, B (1986) 'Beyond Multiculturalism: Towards the Enactment of Anti-Racist Education in Policy, Provision and Pedagogy.' *Oxford Review of Education*, 13 (13), pp.301-320.

Vincent, C (1992). Tolerating Intolerance? Parental choice and race relations-Clevedon Case', *Journal of Education Policy*. 7:5. pp. 429-43.

Vincent, C (1996) *Parents and Teachers: Power and Participation*. London, Falmer.

Vincent, C (2001) Researching Home-School Relations: A Critical Approach. In: *Understanding Learning*. Edited by J. Collins and D. Cook. London, Paul Chapman Press.

Vygotsky, L. S (1978) *Mind in Society: The Development of Higher Psychological Processes*. Cambridge, MA, Harvard University Press.

Waldroph, M, M (1992) *Complexity: The emerging science at the edge of order and chaos*. New York, Simon and Schuster.

Walker, A (2005) Priorities, Strategies and Challenges. In: *Effective Leadership in Multi-Ethnic Schools*. Nottingham, National College for School Leadership.

Walsh, D (1998) Doing Ethnography. In: *Researching Society and Culture*. Edited by C. Seale. London, Sage.

Wilson, A (1978) *Finding a Voice*. London, Virago.

Woods, D.J, Bruner, J.S and Ross, G (1976) The role of tutoring in problem-solving. *Journal of Child Psychology and Psychiatry*, 66, pp. 181-91.

Yonge, C (1998) Investigation into the Ways in which Children Use Collaborative Talk to Develop their Response to Text. Unpublished Thesis, Bath University.

Index